YOU'RE GOING TO DIE SO DO IT ANYWAY

Warning: If you're easily offended, morally outraged by a few swear words, or the kind of judgemental asshole who polices how women should behave after a certain age then kindly shut this book and carry on living your safe, beige little life. This isn't for you.

Still here? Good. That tells me you're one of the few with guts. A spark. A flicker of rebellion under the surface. Maybe you're quietly fed up. Or maybe, like me, you've hit a point in your life where you've thought: "Is this it?" You've ticked all the boxes, played by the rules, been the good girl, the wife, the mother, the employee and now you're looking in the mirror wondering what the fuck happened to the woman you were before you made yourself smaller to fit in.

This book is my middle finger to mediocrity. It's about tearing up the script after 50, starting again, and doing life on your terms no matter what anyone thinks. I left a marriage, rebuilt my body, regained my confidence, and discovered that the second act can be even more thrilling than the first if you've got the balls (or in my case, the boobs) to go for it.

So if you're ready to laugh, cry, wince, and maybe get a kick up the arse in the process turn the page.

Because you're going to die.

So do it anyway.

        Chapter One: Hello New Me

        Chapter Two: Setting Boundaries

        Chapter Three: Fuck being a People Pleaser

        Chapter Four: Health Changes Are Normal

        Chapter Five: Challenge Negative Thoughts

        Chapter Six: The Situationship

        Chapter Seven: Relationships & Sex

        Chapter Eight: The Power of Confidence

        Chapter Nine: Feminism, speak up and create change

        Chapter Ten: SoloTravel

        Chapter Eleven: Financial Fuck Ups

        Chapter Twelve:Personal Growth & New Opportunities

        Chapter Thirteen: 50 is the New 30

        Chapter Fourteen: Live Your Life on Your Terms

Chapter Fifteen: Embrace the Unknown

Chapter Sixteen: Make a Bucket List

CHAPTER ONE: HELLO NEW ME

I have written this book because I am standing up for every woman approaching 50, or in their 50s who are looking at their life and thinking "Is this it?" Have all my cards been dealt on this planet? I am more than a mother and an entrepreneur. I was tired of being an unappreciated wife. I am an energetic person with unfulfilled wants and desires so do I settle for a quiet, sad life or do I embrace the time I have left with gusto, passion, fear and excitement? I am frequently told I am brave and adventurous and that others wish they could do what I do. And I look at them incredulously because I haven't done anything out of the ordinary. I literally just woke up one day and realised I had had enough of the life I was living and wasn't prepared to carry on in the same mediocre monotony for the rest of my life.

Women have on average 27 years left on the planet when they hit 50 so how am I going to live out the rest of my days? Life isn't just about the number of years, it's about the quality of the years and how you live them. At 50, there's still so much potential for growth, joy, and meaningful experiences. You're never too old to start something new. Whether it's learning a new skill, transforming your figure and your style, picking up a hobby, or even switching careers, the possibilities are endless. Many people find some of their most fulfilling experiences later in life and statistically speaking, more women start businesses at the age of 55 and become millionaires.

First of all, I stopped becoming a people pleaser. I learned to say no.

I stopped tolerating mediocre and stopped talking to flaky friends. It can be draining when people only want things their way and aren't flexible or considerate of others. And I stopped pandering to their desires over mine.

I ended my marriage. I looked at my husband and knew I didn't want to be with him, I resented him more and more as the days went on. He left all the responsibilities to me, from the decisions about the kids to running the house, to paying the mortgage and the bills. I felt I was single in a marriage where we weren't an equal partnership. I took the kids on holiday on my own, we never went on date nights and we sat in separate rooms, so I may as well sit in a different house and do what I wanted. It was like I could resonate deeply with women (or anyone) in the same age range who may be questioning how they can make the most of what's ahead. My mindset shift changed my life. Self-care became my priority as I dealt with the stresses of life and I became more selfish. Actually let me rephrase that. Self love became my self care. Okay so my life change may have been a little drastic, I moved abroad from the dreary UK and started a new life in a country where the sun shines for 360 days instead of three. I took myself on holiday to places I always wanted to go.I started a new business, started a fitness regime and dropped 25 kilos. I prioritised my skincare and my happiness.

Sure, I lost friends along the way but they weren't my true friends to begin with. Authentic friends don't disappear when you start standing up for yourself, evolving, or choosing peace over people-pleasing. I set boundaries and let go of perfectionism. I learned to listen to my children's point of view instead of preaching to them. I stopped caring what people thought of me. I said fuck off to people a lot more. I began to live with intention. It's a powerful quality to be able to reflect regularly on my values and goals, ensuring I live in a way that aligns with what's most important to me, instead of just going through the motions. I meditated more and journaled and started talking out loud to the moon, the stars and the universe. And the weirdest part? It answered back.

This isn't some sugar-coated self-help manual. You won't find affirmations and scented candle advice here. What you *will* find is the unfiltered truth about starting over when society says you're "too old" to bother. Fuck that. If you've still got breath in your lungs, you've got time to change your story. A life fulfilled is a life full of changes so hello new you.

Don't be scared because you're going to die.
So do it anyway.

Women in their 50s are a well of wisdom, experience, and strength. We've lived through so many highs, lows, challenges, and triumphs and there's a richness in knowledge that comes from having navigated life's complexities, and that is something that should be celebrated and shared. And yet we're overlooked. At my age I am now at a place where I have gained a deeper understanding of myself and the world around me. I know what matters, what doesn't, and what truly brings fulfillment. This wisdom, along with my unique life experiences, is something that the world can benefit from. I bring a level of emotional intelligence, practical knowledge, and resilience that only time can provide. My life hasn't been easier and I have many battle scars but I have survived and thrived and got the new tattoos to prove it.

Life doesn't always go according to plan and accepting this has been the biggest challenge in my life after the disintegration of my marriage. Doors have closed, and the future has felt uncertain and quite frankly, terrifying. To add to the pile of shit flung at me throughout my existence, I had a situationship breakup which shattered my confidence and tested my decision making for a year. I withdrew inward, barely went out and struggled to trust myself. I felt overwhelmed when things didn't seem to be going my way, as the last two years have been set back after set back. But my enduring resilience and a positive mindset helped me navigate these incredibly difficult times. I have remained unwaveringly strong, hopeful, and now, finally at long last, I am ready to embrace the unknown alone. I am filled with hope and excitement for the possibilities that lie ahead. I am no longer waiting to be saved, chosen, or completed, but trusting myself to write the next chapter on my own terms. And what's the worst that can happen? I could die and then none of it matters anyway.

I have spent my life under stress. Worry is a waste of energy and dwelling on the past won't change your situation, but shifting your focus to what you *can* control will help you move forward with strength and purpose.

Progress is still progress, no matter how small. I celebrated little victories along the way, whether it was writing an email when I couldn't be bothered, or simply maintaining a positive attitude when I was withering inside.

The future is still uncertain for me and I don't have a GPS of where I will end up, but that doesn't mean it won't be a bright destination.. Hard times never last forever, and with perseverance, I am sure exciting opportunities are on the horizon. I have believed in myself when no one else has and I am stronger and more determined than ever. This isn't the first time my security has been shaken. I am incredibly proud of myself for getting this far, fighting for what I believe is right and standing my ground in the face of adversity. Life has a funny way of throwing curveballs but it's how we respond to them that truly matter. My children have been my rock. The love and responsibility I have for them gave me an incredible drive to keep pushing forward.

So this next chapter of my life is going to be my best. I have transformed and I have conquered. I have raised children into magnificent, strong, independent humans. I wasn't born just to get up everyday and sit under a dull, grey clouds, trudging to the supermarket and then sitting at home alone in a little box every night. No, I am going to fulfill all my dreams and I urge you to do the same and will show you how you can do it. No excuses. After all, you're going to die so you may as well do it anyway.

CHAPTER TWO: SETTING BOUNDARIES

Boundaries. A simple word that can carry a profound impact in your life. It's one of those things that seems easy to understand in theory, but putting it into practice often feels like navigating a maze. Boundaries aren't just about saying "no" to people—they're about saying "yes" to yourself. They are the invisible lines we draw to protect our energy, our time, and our well-being. When done right, they allow us to show up as our best selves, both for others and for ourselves. It's about protecting your peace. Boundaries matter. I was finding as I was getting older that I was slipping into wallpaper syndrome. I was around but people weren't taking notice of me and I had so much to say. The husband ignored me. I was invisible to the kids. My business clients wanted to speak to be well into the night, and demanded a reply even if they messaged me at 11pm. I was emotionally exhausted and incredibly isolated. I was always there for everyone else but never there for me. When you're in the background for so long, it's easy to feel like you've lost your voice or that what you have to say doesn't matter. But it *does* matter.

When I look back on my life so far I didn't have any boundaries. I let my mother push me around, I let her slap me, tell me I was fat and useless and that I didn't deserve to be loved. I let her lock me out of the house and make me walk the streets for hours as a kid and then return home for more abuse. It was only until I reached my 20s did I finally tell her to fuck off and get out of my life.

All of my childhood, like every little girl, I dreamed of a beautiful wedding in a gorgeous gown acting like a princess for the day. The reality was a marriage proposal from him telling me to "book the registry" office while he was on the toilet and I was wailing to him that car insurance would be cheaper if we were married. The wedding was dull, we drove ourselves to the registry office and he couldn't even be arsed to put a ribbon on the car. Then we came home, had a buffet in the house and I went off to bed to feed Saxon who was 5 months old. And as for the honeymoon? I am saving that romantic getaway for my second marriage.

The fact is that back then I didn't have boundaries and set low standards for myself. And the first step in stepping out of wallpaper syndrome was reclaiming my voice. This didn't mean shouting over others or demanding constant attention, although it's true I did both. It means reminding yourself that you have a perspective, ideas, and feelings that are just as valuable as anyone else's. Don't wait for permission: You might feel like you need someone to acknowledge you before you speak up, but part of reclaiming your voice is to speak up *for yourself* first. Your thoughts, opinions, and presence are valid, even if no one else notices right away.

Here's the thing: you *are* worthy of being seen and heard, and it's totally okay to want and demand attention, respect, and meaningful connection from the people around you, especially your family. The fact that you're noticing this now is a powerful first step. It means you're still in touch with your needs and ready to make changes.

Imagine being a phone with a constantly draining battery. You can't give more than what you have. If you don't recharge, you'll eventually stop working altogether. Setting boundaries is how you recharge. They allow you to conserve your energy so you can engage with the world in a way that feels sustainable. Without boundaries, you risk burnout, resentment, and ultimately, losing touch with what makes you *you*.

Boundaries help clarify expectations. They help others understand what you need and where your limits are, making it easier for them to interact with you respectfully. And ultimately, they lead to healthier relationships because they foster mutual understanding.

But why is it so difficult for many of us to establish and enforce boundaries? Part of the reason is that we're conditioned to prioritize others. Especially as mothers and wives. For so many years in my marriage I used to blow my top at the sheer frustration of my life. I would leave my babies and go to work, miserable in the existence that they were home without me, often for ten hours a day whilst I earned the money to pay the bills. Then when I arrived home I would be berated for the kitchen being messy, or leaving the plates in the sink. I would be on the receiving end of silent treatment for days if I didn't attend to my husband's desires. I found myself walking on eggshells. As I wanted to be closer to my young children I allowed them to sleep in my bed and my husband moved into his own room. He never moved back into the bedroom and sex became a chore. There was no romance, no appreciation of me and no affection. I comfort ate junk food and lived a lonely existence. I still resent the fact that I never received a push present for giving birth to six beautiful babies. Twice I had to get a taxi to the hospital myself in labour. I felt unloved, a common feeling from childhood and it was incredibly painful, and it made everything else feel heavier.

I now know I am worthy of love and care, even if it feels like it's not showing up right now. The universe doesn't work on timing we can control. we can control. It works on alignment, growth, and trust. What's meant for me is making its way to me, even in the silence, even in the stillness. Sometimes, love is just harder to see or find, but it doesn't mean it's not there.

Another boundary is friendships.So often my friends at the time would call me and ask me how I was and without waiting for my reply they would then enter into a monologue of their dramatic lives. I got bored of listening to one way conversations. I started to question if they would miss me if I wasn't around and I came to the conclusion that they probably wouldn't. So I stopped answering the phone to them and made excuses not to see them until I eventually said no. We're taught that being kind means saying "yes," even when it goes against our own needs. We worry about disappointing others, feeling guilty about turning down requests, or fearing we'll be seen as selfish. But the truth is, boundaries are not selfish—they are necessary. And it is so fucking liberating to hang up on people and cut them out of your life.

I realised this as I approached my 50th birthday, that my happiness was being forfeited at the expense of others. I regularly escaped to my Cyprus holiday home. My sanctuary, my peace and used to cry when I returned home. Until eventually one day, my older teenage children suggested I stay there, not because they didn't want me around, but because they knew I was happier there and they didn't want to see me sad anymore. And so I looked into moving permanently and replicating my business model over there. This was the first stage of me setting boundaries. I realised as I was getting older that I had to put myself and my needs first if I was to create a happier life for myself.

Physical boundaries are the most obvious and tangible boundaries. They relate to your personal space, physical comfort, and how much contact you're willing to have with others.. These boundaries are essential for creating a sense of safety and comfort in your physical environment. My walls are so high right now that I am untouchable, except to my kids whom I have endless hugs for.

Emotional boundaries are perhaps the trickiest because they relate to your emotional energy. They help you manage how much emotional investment you're willing to give to others. These boundaries protect you from becoming emotionally overwhelmed or taking on other people's emotional baggage. For instance, it might mean not engaging in negative or toxic conversations or distancing yourself from relationships that consistently drain you. I gave up on friends who would call me only to talk about themselves. Friends who called me to listen to them cry over their problems and not once ask about my life or how I was feeling. My boundary is now refusing to absorb other people's negativity or drama. I will not be manipulated or pressured into adopting other people's views, especially when those views conflict with my own. This is why I haven't watched the news for years. I also came off X which is rife with racism and politics I don't align with. News is just a cycle of negativity and stress. If it doesn't add value to my life, why let it take up space in my mind? I have been a member of the media for 35 years, I know stories are published to create a knee jerk reaction to get you to engage with it. I abstained.

Time is our most valuable resource, yet many of us give it away without considering the cost. Time boundaries are about protecting your time and using it wisely. It might look like scheduling downtime, limiting how much time you spend on non-essentials, or saying no to commitments that don't align with your values. When you set time boundaries, you create space for the things that truly matter. I stopped showing up to meetings I didn't want to go to. I stopped accepting invitations to the opening of an envelope with business. I stopped saying yes to every pointless business event. Honestly, strike me down with lightning, but I *loathe* networking gatherings. I can't stand the forced camaraderie and fake small talk which is heightened on LinkedIn. If I see one more post starting with "I am excited to announce…." I might actually scream. No one gives a shit except you and that's fine but to brag on a platform designed to make others feel insignificantly less successful than you fills my mouth with a little bit of sick.

The biggest hurdle to setting boundaries is fear. Fear of rejection. Fear of conflict. Fear of being seen as difficult or cold-hearted. I actually couldn't give a shit. I am more scared of settling into a life I hate with people who bore me and don't stimulate me. The truth is, you might encounter resistance when you first start establishing boundaries. People might try to push past them, ignore them, or make you feel guilty and boy did I feel guilty but then I stopped caring what other people thought of me. Their opinions are their issues, not mine. They don't pay my bills or bring me peace so why should they matter?

Before you can set boundaries, you must understand where your limits are. I began to identify areas of my life where I felt overwhelmed, stressed, or undervalued. I didn't like aspects of my job. Being self employed and constantly chasing invoices for work I had done, I was made to feel like I was harassing people for what I was owed. People wouldn't reply to my polite requests for payment. I did always get paid in the end but refused to work with them again. One time, and quite recently, I had a client who asked to appear on the cover of my magazine. I told him the price he agreed to and arranged to interview him at his place of work. I turned up with my phone to record the interview. He turned up an hour late with no excuse or apology. I only hung around because his business overlooked the beach so I relaxed for an hour whilst waiting. I conducted the interview, with questions he had previously approved. I went away and wrote up the interview, almost word for word from the aural notes and sent it to him for approval. He emailed me saying he didn't like the interview and was unhappy with the feature. He actually questioned my integrity so I told him to fuck off. I could have remained polite with him for fear of losing a client but no, he had disrespected my time, for making me wait for him. He disrespected my intelligence for criticizing my integrity and he disrespected my business which I have years building up. I received an email a few days later from him apologising, telling me he was all alone running a business and he was feeling the pressure. Like, that's not my problem, so am I. And I am 3000 miles away from my children trying to earn a living, all alone but I was still conducting myself with dignity and professionalism. And yes, it was a man of course. Another one useless with his emotional intelligence.

Boundaries are not meant to be demands or ultimatums. They're simply statements about your needs. I don't need to apologize or justify my boundaries, they're just facts. After a lifetime of putting everyone else's needs first it's time to concentrate on mine. It's ok to say, "I'm unable to help with this right now, I need to focus on my own work" or "I can only stay for an hour, I have other commitments." And remember, don't apologise, you're just showing respect for yourself. Your value is more important than someone else' needs or opinions.

You don't owe anyone an explanation for your boundaries. "No" is a complete sentence. You don't need to give an elaborate backstory to justify your decisions. I never explain. No is no. It is simple and firm reduces room for negotiation or guilt-tripping. I have lost count of the number of times unknown men on social media have slid into my DMs asking to meet me. Usually they're ignored or blocked but occasionally, if I am bored and lacking human contact for a while, I reply with a no.

Why? They ask. Because I said so. That is enough.

Saying "no" is a skill that requires practice. Start small, like saying no to minor requests, and build your confidence over time. It will feel awkward at first, but the more you do it, the easier it becomes and once you master it, it becomes a superpower

I discovered that once I started setting boundaries, I noticed people shrank away and called me less and less and that was fine. Lovely in fact. I was committed to me and my happiness first I stood firm in my decision. If someone challenges my boundary, remind yourself that their discomfort is temporary, but your peace is non-negotiable.

Setting boundaries was a gamechanger for me and a beginning of my self-love era. It all started when I left my husband. I was sick of his skulking around the house and refusing to get a job. I resented that he slept in until lunchtime while I got up and got the kids ready for school and then began work on my business. I hated him for criticising that the house wasn't tidy when, ironically, it was filled with all his shit and clutter. I stopped fancying him, sex became a chore and when I didn't follow his demands I was on the receiving end of his silent treatment for days. It wore me down and occasionally I would give in to keep the peace. But it wasn't my peace. I began to say no and by doing so I was raising my standards of how I expected to be treated. I created a space for for deeper, more fulfilling relationships which is still waiting to be filled. But I won't settle anymore. Boundaries are not walls that isolate you; they're the gates that protect the things most important to you—your time, your energy, and your well-being.

By making boundaries a non-negotiable part of your life, you take control of how you show up in the world. You protect your peace, honor your needs, and, in turn, allow yourself to live a more authentic, fulfilling life. Remember, boundaries are an act of self-respect.

When you set yourself boundaries you open yourself up to live your life your way. You give yourself the freedom to live life on your own terms. You stop bending to others' expectations and start prioritizing what truly matters to you. Boundaries aren't about shutting people out—they're about making space for the right energy, opportunities, and experiences. The moment you stop apologizing for protecting your time, peace, and happiness, you open the door to a life that feels authentic and fulfilling, creating a life that you love without limits.

CHAPTER THREE: STOP BEING A PEOPLE PLEASER

For so many of us, the desire to please others can feel like an ingrained part of who we are. It's as if we've been taught from a young age that our worth is tied to how much we give, how much we sacrifice, and how much we make others happy. But here's the hard truth: constantly trying to please others at the expense of your own well-being doesn't lead to happiness. It leads to burnout, resentment, and a loss of your sense of self.

I only realised as I approached 50, that being a people-pleaser can hold you back. It's exhausting to put the brakes on it but essentially, once you find your strength and reclaim your power by learning to put your own needs first, everything changes and a beautiful life awaits. It's time to stop living for others and start living for YOU.

People-pleasing is the habit of constantly trying to make others happy, often at the expense of your own needs, desires, and values. It's about seeking external validation, fearing conflict, and avoiding disappointment, even when it means sacrificing your time, energy, and mental health. As mothers we're expected to put our needs last, and this is completely natural when our kids are very young, I accept that it is ok to pause your needs. Your every attention is poured into their priorities. But a problem arises when self sacrifice develops into a lifelong habit and you find yourself slipping into wallpaper syndrome. It often happens in long-term relationships, workplaces, or social circles where someone feels they've blended into the background, losing their sense of individuality or significance. By the time I had reached 40, this was me, fat, ugly, unhappy and overlooked. Taken for granted in every way. Looking back, I was a people pleaser in my business, wanting everyone to like me so that they would work with me. As I transformed and told people gleefully to fuck off, my client list shrank but I was far more happier and fulfilled as I stepped into my spotlight. That's a win for me. And if you're reading this and you used to know me, and I haven't spoken to you recently, it's because I don't want to.

At its core, people-pleasing stems from a fear of rejection or disapproval. I spent my entire childhood being rejected by both parents. My father walked out when I was three years old and didn't return until I was 35 years old, when he fleetingly revisited my life to steal my life savings. As I have mentioned before, my narcissistic mother spent my entire childhood telling me that I didn't deserve to be loved and she wished I was dead and that I was too fat and was an idiot. So I had a deep rooted desire to be accepted by everyone. My mother would start physical fights with me for no reason and I learned to say yes to her, even if I disagreed, just to keep her calm. I was conditioned to believe that love and approval are earned through self-sacrifice and a desire to avoid conflict or criticism as well as a deep-seated fear of being unloved or rejected. When I was a teenager I was renting a room in a flat in London and my mother turned up unannounced and I invited her in. My friends were with me and she cornered my friend in the bathroom and blocked the doorway so she couldn't get past. My mother then proceeded to grill her as to why she wanted to be friends with me and she could do better. No wonder I was desperate to be popular and be seen in large social circles. So, I gave and gave, sometimes to the point of exhaustion, all in an effort to maintain approval and avoid conflict. Ironically now, I wouldn't be seen dead in those circles.

It's funny to observe that while people-pleasing may temporarily provide you with a sense of acceptance or praise, it's never a sustainable source of happiness. The truth is, the more you try to please others, the less you end up pleasing yourself. Over time, you lose sight of your own needs and become a shell of the person you were meant to be. Saying NO is the most powerful thing you can ever do and you will thank me for it.

When I was married I never got my nails or hair done, I was told botox was for sad people desperate to cling onto their youth and I listened because I didn't want to offend anyone. But I was pandering to the whim of my husband who either didn't want me to look my best for anyone else or simply didn't want me to spend money on what he thought was triviality.

There are many reasons why we fall into the habit of people-pleasing, and often, it starts in childhood. We may have learned that love and approval are earned through self-sacrifice. It could stem from a desire to avoid conflict or criticism, or a deep-seated fear of being unloved or rejected. Social conditioning also plays a role, as women, in particular, are often socialized to be caretakers, nurturers, and peacekeepers.

For many, there is also an underlying guilt. Guilt about saying "no" to someone. Guilt about taking time for yourself. Guilt about setting boundaries, because we fear letting others down or disappointing them.

But the truth is, constantly prioritizing others above yourself doesn't make you a better person. It makes you exhausted. When you are so focused on satisfying the needs of others, you lose touch with your own desires and values. You can't pour from an empty cup, and the more you give without replenishing, the more disconnected you become from your true self.

People-pleasing might feel like a way to gain love and approval, but it comes with significant emotional and mental costs:

Over time, I began to feel resentful. I resenteed the people I was trying to please, and I hated myself for not standing up for my needs. I felt taken advantage of and exhausted because I was constantly giving without receiving.

Persistently putting others first means you often lose touch with who you really are and what you want. You might find yourself saying yes to things you don't want to do or agreeing to compromises that don't align with your values.

People-pleasing takes physical and emotional energy. When you're always doing for others, you neglect your own self-care. This can lead to burnout, anxiety, and a sense of being overwhelmed. When you're always putting others' needs before your own, you can attract people who take advantage of your kindness, leaving you feeling drained and unappreciated. Healthy relationships are built on mutual respect and care, not one-sided sacrifices.

You can't grow if you're constantly looking outside of yourself for validation. True growth comes from learning to trust your own instincts, making decisions based on your desires, and stepping into your authentic power. People-pleasing keeps you stuck in a cycle of external validation.

The first step in stopping the cycle of people-pleasing is recognizing and acknowledging the patterns. Ask yourself how often you say yes when instead you're screaming the opposite? How often do you put other people's needs before your own, when it's inconvenient or draining? Is the fear of rejection worth sacrificing your own peace? Of course not.

People-pleasing is not about being kind or compassionate, it's about self-sacrifice in unhealthy ways. It's important to understand that your worth is not dependent on how much you can do for others. You are worthy of love and respect simply for being YOU.

Learning to say no is one of the most empowering skills you can develop. When you say no to something that doesn't serve you, you're saying "yes" to your own well-being. You're taking control of your time, your energy, and your life. You're honoring your own needs and setting clear boundaries. I learnt to say no to living in the UK. I hate the country,

I hate the politics, I hate the weather, I hate the lifestyle, I hate everything about the country.

People-pleasing often stems from a belief that our worth is based on how much we can give to others. But true self-worth comes from within. You are worthy because you exist, not because you're constantly meeting everyone else's needs.

Journaling was a brilliant way for me to increase my self-esteem by affirming my value every day. Now I end every night writing down five things that make me uniquely me. I also do not go to sleep without listing ten things I am grateful for that day. My strengths, my talents, my kindness, my creativity. I celebrate those things even if no one else does. I have embraced my worth and realize that I am more than enough just as I am.

Let's address the guilt now. One of the hardest parts of stopping people-pleasing is letting go of the guilt that comes with it. You may feel guilty for saying no, for taking time for yourself, or for not meeting everyone's expectations. But guilt is not a sign that you're doing something wrong, it's simply a reflection of old conditioning. Yes, I felt guilty for moving away from my kids. Of course I did. I'm a mother, not a monster. But I've let go of that guilt now. My children love me, and they understand. Guilt is a waste of space. It serves no one, and certainly not the woman I've fought to become.

Reclaim your power. Learn to say no, embrace your worth, set boundaries, and release the guilt. When you stop being a people-pleaser, you stop giving your power away, and you start living a life that's authentic, fulfilling, and yours.

CHAPTER FOUR: CHALLENGE NEGATIVE THOUGHTS

Every woman, at some point in her life, has been caught in the grip of negative thoughts. Whether they arise from past experiences, societal expectations, or our own internal doubts, these thoughts can often feel like a heavy weight we can't shake off. They tell us we're not good enough, not skinny enough, not worthy enough, or that we will never succeed. But here's the truth: these negative thoughts do not define us. They do not have the power to control our futures unless we allow them to. And social media doesn't help when we're bombarded daily with ideal body images and unrealistic beauty goals.

The menopause was cruel to me. Limiting beliefs started to creep in and I had to learn how to replace them with empowering, self-affirming thoughts that align with the powerful women that I truly am. Honestly I have spent days wondering if I wanted to live anymore sometimes.

Many women may internalize the idea that menopause signifies the end of vitality, desirability, or productivity, leading to self-doubt and diminished confidence. Symptoms like brain fog, horrendous mood swings, or fatigue can reinforce these beliefs, making it easy to feel incapable or irrelevant. However, overcoming these limitations starts with reframing menopause as a transition rather than an endpoint. Embracing self-care, seeking support, and focusing on strengths such as wisdom, resilience, and experience, can shift the narrative. I practiced mindfulness, and living in Cyprus, I took advantage of going to the beach everyday to calm my negative thoughts, and I engaged in activities that brought me joy and fulfillment. For me this was the gym. This helped me reclaim their power. I toned up and became physically stronger and I saw a noticeable decline in my physical aging. So much so that people began to tell me I looked ten years younger. I began to see the menopause as a time of renewal and self-discovery rather than decline.

It's easy to let those negative thoughts creep in, especially as we get older and they are often rooted in fear. Fear of failure, fear of judgment, or fear of not meeting expectations. I worried that my kids thought I was a failure, I worried that they would resent me for moving abroad. I worried that I would never meet anyone and spend the rest of my life alone. I worried that I wasn't good enough in general and now my kids were growing up and leading their own lives, that I was becoming surplus to their needs. Over time, if we don't challenge these thoughts, they can shape our self-perception and limit our potential. The harsh voice in your head that says, *"You're not enough,"* or *"You'll never make it,"* is not the voice of truth. It's the voice of fear and doubt, and it's time to recognize it for what it is.

I began to understand that negative thinking is a natural human response. Our brains are wired to protect us from danger, but sometimes, this instinctual self-protection becomes overactive. Our minds start to associate even small risks or challenges with feelings of danger. In those moments, we need to pause and consciously challenge these thoughts.

The first step in challenging negative thoughts is awareness. You cannot change what you do not see. Throughout your day, notice when you have self-doubting or critical thoughts. Maybe it's in the middle of a meeting when you wonder if your ideas are good enough, or when you're about to speak in public and hear that voice telling you, *"You're going to mess up."*

Once I recognised the thought, the next step is to challenge it. I had to make myself ask: *"Is this thought based on facts? Is this really true?"* Often, when you dig a little deeper, you'll realize that your negative thoughts are not grounded in reality. They're assumptions, fears, or beliefs that you've carried with you for years, often without questioning their validity. And how much energy is wasted on useless negative thoughts?

I find a great way to get myself out of this is to ask myself, what would I say to my son or daughter having the same thought. Of course I would remind them of all the incredible things they have achieved. You and I deserve that same level of kindness and understanding. I have a list on my phone in my notes of 25 things I am proud of and things I have achieved and I often turn to this list when the chatter in my head starts.

Once you've challenged the negative thought, it's time to reframe it. Reframing is the process of seeing the situation from a new perspective. Instead of looking at it through the lens of fear and doubt, look at it through the lens of possibility and opportunity.

For instance, if you're thinking, *"I always fail at everything I try,"* reframe that thought into something like, *"I have faced challenges before, and each time, I learned and grew stronger. This is just another opportunity for me to learn and rise."*

Reframing helps shift the focus from your limitations to your strengths. It empowers you to see the challenges in your life as stepping stones rather than roadblocks.

One of the most powerful ways to challenge negative thoughts is to use affirmations. Affirmations are positive statements that reinforce your worth, power, and capabilities. They are a tool to reprogram your subconscious mind and change the narrative you've been telling yourself.

Affirmations have become my best friend as I reclaim the narrative in my head that reflects my truth and the woman I became. And remember that no matter where you are today, in six months time you can look back and think that really was all just a storm in a teacup. Some examples of empowering affirmations are:

- *"I am worthy of success and happiness."*
- *"I am capable, confident, and powerful."*
- *"I embrace challenges as opportunities for growth."*
- *"I am enough, just as I am."*

As I do regularly, the more you repeat these affirmations, the more your mindset will shift. Over time, they will begin to replace the negative thoughts that once held you back. And whenever I feel like i am spiralling, i srop and breathe and remember the affirmations to remind myself that all is well.

Youtube and inspirational podcasts from the likes of Mel Robbins became my best friend when these thoughts crept in. I would find meditations and positive sounds waves from Inner Lotus Music which helped frame my thoughts and allowed me to see these obstacles as opportunities for growth. I talked myself out of limiting beliefs with affirmations like, *"I am capable, and I will overcome this"*. It's the old phrase, thoughts become things

Challenging negative thoughts isn't just about changing your inner dialogue; it's also about taking action. Often, negative thoughts keep us stuck in a state of inaction because we're afraid of failing. But the only way to truly grow and conquer fear is to take action, even if it's imperfect.

The more you act, the more proof you'll gather that you are capable. Every step, however small, is a victory. Action builds confidence, and confidence silences the inner critic.

In conclusion you're more powerful than you think. And actually it's something that my personal trainer says to me all the time when I lift weights. Our bodies are meant to be strong and so are our minds. Challenging negative thoughts is a lifelong practice, but it's a practice that will empower you to step into the fullness of who you are. Remember that every thought you think has the potential to shape your reality. So, why not choose thoughts that lift you up, fuel your dreams, and remind you of your worth?

The journey to reclaiming your power starts with your mind. When you challenge negative thoughts, you make room for your true strength to shine through. You are worthy, capable, and deserving of all the success and happiness you desire. Trust that the power to create your best life lies within you.

Now is the time to break free from self-doubt, embrace your limitless potential, and step forward into the life you deserve. You've got this. And if anyone tries to bring you down or piss on your parade, tell them to fuck off.

CHAPTER FIVE: HEALTH CHANGES ARE NORMAL

Us women in our 50s experience a unique phase in life, where health, well-being, and personal growth take on a new level of importance. Our bodies are always changing—aging, evolving, and adapting. The moment we're born, we're already moving toward the end, so why waste time worrying about things that are out of our control? Instead of letting menopause or any other life stage hold us back, it's a reminder to do whatever makes us happy, chase what excites us, and live on our own terms. Life is short, and there's no point in spending it listening to the negative chatter or confirming to society's expectations of us at 50.

I know I repeat myself — but if you're reading this, it's because you're looking for something. A nudge. A sign. Some real, grounded guidance from someone who's been through the shit and comes out stronger on the other side. And here's the thing: repetition isn't annoying, it's essential. I work in advertising and I always tell my clients that one advert will be a waste of time. It will be ignored. Two adverts and someone may recognise it but repetition is key for it to be memorable and it's the same with the negative thoughts. Why do you keep seeing the same adverts on the TV or hear the same adverts eight times a day on the radio? We don't absorb information the first time we hear it. We need to hear it again, and again, until it drowns out the bullshit we've been fed for decades. So yes, I'll keep banging the same drum: you are not too old, it is not too late, and you don't need anyone's permission to start over. I turned 48. I left the old me behind. I embarked on a rigorous fitness plan, dropped 25 kilos, got hair extensions, lash extensions, botox and transformed myself physically. I completely took control of my life and reinvented myself on my own terms! It takes serious dedication to commit to that level of transformation, and five years on, the gym is a non-negotiable part of my daily routine and has taught me self respect. I am now fitter than I ever was and have the fitness levels of a 39 year old. That's badass! I have proved that age is just a number and that with the right mindset and discipline, you can be in the best shape of your life at any stage. My body has changed: I have noticed my metabolism has slowed down with age, and fat distribution changes. My belly has a mind of its own and after a lifetime of hating it, I started to love it and be grateful for it. After all, it did grow six healthy and amazing babies, which is what it was designed for. I have embraced my curves as a natural part of aging and focused on being healthy, not just a certain size or shape. And I'm not competing with women half my age. The posts I see on social media can be so damaging but remember, these posts are often filters and create so many unrealistic standards. Instead I focus on being the best version of *myself*. Confidence, strength, and self-acceptance are way more powerful than chasing an illusion. It's time to embrace who you are, without the societal pressures of youth and beauty. And to celebrate this I got four tattoos at 50 to celebrate myself. The first was a tiger on my arm, which symbolises strength and fierceness as well as being ruthlessly protective of my babies. The second was a giant scorpio woman with a sting in her tail, across my hip and thigh. The third was wonderwoman on my opposite thigh, as that is who I transformed into and the final tattoo was a bleeding rose shedding tears on my back, to symbolise all the tears I have cried over people who have stabbed me in the back but will not be allowed to do so anymore.

I told my exhusband that menopause was affecting my hormones and he rolled his eyes. Not the first time he was so dismissive over something so life changing. Menopause is the biggest effect on a woman's body after puberty and pregnancy. We experience changes in menstrual cycles, hot flashes, and sleep disturbances. Hormonal therapy or natural remedies can help alleviate some symptoms but I refuse to take any for fear of gaining weight. Meditation is my medication.

As we get older our estrogen levels decrease, bone density may decline, increasing the risk of osteoporosis. Weight-bearing exercises and a calcium-rich diet are important to keep bones strong which is why I go to the gym everyday. Strong is sexy and I am less likely to fall over and break a bone with a strong core.

The risk of heart disease increases after menopause, so managing cholesterol, blood pressure, and maintaining a healthy weight is crucial which all leads me back to the gym to monitor it all.

As we approach 50 we experience a boost in self-acceptance and self-assurance. It's a time to embrace who you are, without the societal pressures of youth and beauty. Getting the chance to grow old is a gift and a privilege, many of us don't even make it this far.

Engaging in mentally stimulating activities, like reading, puzzles, and learning new things, can help keep your brain sharp. There are many games on your phone app to help you.

Our role as a parent changes as children become adults and leave the nest. I swear it's weird being at my family home in Liverpool with half my kids away travelling in Thailand. I feel like I am rattling around the walls and I miss their laughter and the aroma of the five different meals they cook each night.But at the same time i am happy that i have brought them up to be independent with a lust for life. Surrounding yourself with a supportive network of friends is crucial because while your kids are off doing their thing, you can feel redundant and at a loose end. Now is the time to cultivate deeper, more meaningful relationships for yourself that bring joy and fulfillment.

CHAPTER SIX: THE SITUATIONSHIP

After I left my marriage, I didn't fall in love. I fell into fire. It was fast, intoxicating, magnetic, the kind of connection that lights you up and blinds you at the same time. A passionate situationship that felt like escape, like rebirth, like proof that I was still desirable, still alive. It had been 25 years since I had slept with another man and I never thought I would. It was exhilarating, exciting and all consuming.

But what I didn't see at the time was how thin the line is between chemistry and chaos. He was charming, yes but also cruel. Belittling in a way that's hard to put your finger on. Sarcastic compliments, Putting down my business, saying I didn't do any real work. All subtle digs disguised as humour or concern, chipping away at my confidence while pretending to be supportive. It was manipulation wrapped in charm, designed to make me doubt my worth and question my success. Silent punishments, little jabs that made me question myself. And bit by bit, without realising it, I began to shrink again. I softened my voice. I tolerated things I screamed about in my marriage..I let boundaries blur, not because I didn't have any, but because I wanted to be loved and desired so badly, I started to forget my own worth.

I thought I was in control. But really, I was just lost again. This time in someone else's storm. I accepted breadcrumb affection. I tolerated low-level cruelty and piss taking masked as banter. I allowed yet another man to dim my light to keep his shining. I will never lose myself like that again. Again, my boundaries were skewered. But I've learned passion isn't the same as respect. Intensity isn't the same as intimacy. And being wanted doesn't mean being valued.

Now, my standards are sky high.
Not for how someone looks but for how they speak to me.
How they show up.
How they honour my boundaries.
How they make me feel when I'm not naked and smiling.

That situationship taught me what I will never tolerate again. Funnily enough it was a word he used to describe me. I was "intolerable" to him. But really I was just a woman with a voice who wasn't prepared to be quiet. I have an opinion and I wasn't afraid to express it. I understand that *intolerable* often just means "a woman who won't tolerate nonsense." It means I have boundaries, standards, and a voice I'm no longer afraid to use. If that makes me too much for him, then he was never enough for me. The situationship was a hard, necessary lesson and I don't regret it. Because from that place of chaos, I found a fiercer kind of self-love. One with teeth. One with a spine. I am certain he has found less with someone else.

It didn't end with a dramatic goodbye. It ended quietly by text with a message "I don't find you sexually attractive". And then I was blocked like I never existed. Erased in a second. That was heartbreak in its most cowardly form. Cruel, cutting, and deliberately designed to wound and it says everything about *him*, not me.

That text was completely unnecessary. And for a while, it did exactly what he wanted it to: it made me question my worth. My body. My desirability. Everything I had been slowly rebuilding since my marriage ended. I cried for a year. But here's what I know now: When someone tries to destroy you with words, it's because they already feel powerless.

That text wasn't the truth. I know I'm gorgeous. It was a last attempt to humiliate me, to regain control in a dynamic where I was fiercely independent and living my life freely. I wasn't a slave to a corporation, I was self employed and a digital nomad working from the beach and wasn't tied to anything. He resented my freedom and my resistance to conformity.

He tried to break me but here's the thing, I am unbreakable. Yes I fell apart briefly and I needed that time to cry and to heal. But the woman I am now doesn't stay on the floor. She reads that text, wipes her tears, and writes a book. That man doesn't get the final word. He most certainly doesn't get to define my beauty, my physical strength, my worth, or my sexuality.

Because I am all of those things not for his approval, but because I *say so*. His rejection was a gift in disguise.

Hurting a woman who was already hurting is where he failed not just as a man but as a human being. At the time I was emotional, carrying the guilt of leaving my children and moving abroad and silently fighting battles he never knew. I was struggling to hold myself together and instead of providing comfort, he gave me confusion. When I would get close he would pull away. He didn't see pain, he added to it and instead of providing protection, he gave me another reason to protect myself and make my shield even more durable.

The situationship reminded me to never again let someone else's opinion overwrite my own truth. It reminded me that silence is stronger than reaction. And it gave me something he never had and that is healthy boundaries. I am now filled with excitement at the prospect of falling in love for real next time with someone who will reciprocate. I have so much love to give to the right person.

So thank you for the text. Because it led me right back to myself.

The situationship let me heal from falling into the same pattern of finding low-value men who were threatened by my light and tried to dim it. Men who couldn't handle the fullness of who I am so they belittled, controlled, or ghosted instead. These men weren't strong, they were *insecure*. And rather than rise to meet me, they tried to pull me down to their level. That's not love. That's emotional sabotage.

I ignored red flags because I wanted connection. I dropped boundaries because I craved intimacy. I gave chances to men who hadn't even earned my time let alone my heart. But I see it now. And I forgive myself. Never again. I would rather be joyfully single than ever again shrink myself to fit into a man's limited idea of what a woman should be. I no longer chase love. I attract it by standing fully in who I am. I am powerful, opinionated, glamorous, curvy, loud, bold, brilliant. If someone can't handle me at full strength, they're not my person. I am no longer explaining, performing, softening, or apologising.

I don't just deserve respect, I expect it. From anyone who enters my life, romantically or otherwise. I am not too much. They were simply not enough.

CHAPTER SEVEN: RELATIONSHIPS AND SEX

After leaving my marriage, I didn't tiptoe into my new life. I ran at it barefoot, tits out in the sunshine, and unapologetically free. I embraced a hedonistic lifestyle in the sunshine, and for the first time in years, I felt alive in every sense of the word. I said yes to pleasure, yes to passion, and yes to men who made me laugh and sometimes made me breakfast. I lost a few friends along the way, but fuck them. They weren't really friends, just spectators who got uncomfortable watching me shine. Jealousy is a bitter pill, and I refused to swallow it. This chapter of my life wasn't about playing it safe. It was about reclaiming my body, my desires, and my right to enjoy both without guilt.

These days, my life revolves around me catching planes like buses back and forth between Cyprus and the UK to see my kids. It's a rhythm that works for us all. I get sunshine, space, and freedom, and they get a mum who's finally alive and actually enjoying life and not just enduring it.

I'll never forget the time I bumped into an old acquaintance in Tesco. Our kids had been in the same class at school, but as they grew older and we realised we had nothing else in common, we drifted apart. Truthfully, I always felt small in her company — she had a way of making you feel like you were somehow failing at life if you didn't have the right handbag or bake the perfect PTA cupcakes. So there I was, fresh off a flight, sun-kissed, glowing, and reaching for a bag of spinach when she came charging up to me like a scene out of *Brookside*.

"OMG, Amanda, you look A-M-A-Z-I-N-G!" she shrieked in her thick Scouse accent. "Tell me your secret!"

I smiled sweetly, tossed back my long hair extensions and said, "Fucking a 38-year-old man." Watching her smile crumble was absolutely priceless.

That's the thing about reinvention, it always pisses someone else off.

I haven't found the grand love story I secretly (or not-so-secretly) crave. Not yet. No candlelit slow dances under the stars, no poetic confessions from some rugged silver fox who sees my soul. But what I have found is adventure. Freedom. And a hell of a good time auditioning men along the way.

Along my journey, I also found sun-drenched flings, late-night conversations and cocktails that ended in tangled sheets, and a few men who couldn't quite believe their luck. I was 50, fierce, and finally putting my pleasure at the centre of the story. Some men couldn't handle that. Others eagerly applied to the task.

Sure, none of them have stuck, not in the deep, soulful way I'd like. And yes, there have been moments I've felt lonely, even in a crowded bar or next to a man who thought a goodnight kiss was the same as connection. But I wouldn't trade the journey. Each one was an experience. Most of them forgettable, one or two unforgettable but all of them part of the process of me becoming *more* myself.

Because here's the truth: I may still be waiting for love. But I haven't wasted a second. And funnily enough, for the last year I have chosen to be celibate, to concentrate on ME and work out what I want in the future. Stepping away from distractions has given me the clarity to understand what I truly want in a partner and in my future. This part of my life hasn't been about absence; it's been about present and fully showing up for myself.

Last year I was by the pool in my complex, minding my own business in a string bikini with the sun on my skin, drink in hand, living my best life when one of the frumpy, bitter ex-pat women waddled over and sneered, "I know the kind of woman you are." Oh really, love? Enlighten me. Apparently, she'd taken it upon herself to try and ban me from wearing bikinis, putting up posters around the pool that sunbathing topless was against her self imposed rules. She convinced herself I was going to pounce on her husband. As if he wasn't two sandals away from a coronary and glued to Sky Sports. The delusion was almost admirable. I'm not after anyone's beer-bellied husband. If I want company, I can find myself a young stud who actually knows how to keep up. But what really got under her skin wasn't my swimwear, it was the fact that I was confident, single, and still owning my sexuality. That kind of freedom terrifies women who've long since handed theirs over.

While some women's libidos pack a suitcase and head off into early retirement at the first sign of menopause, mine, like many other women our age, stepped right into the spotlight. Hot flashes? Yes. Mood swings? Occasionally. But the fire in my belly? Burning brighter than ever. It's like my body finally clocked that time is precious, and instead of winding down, it decided to double down on pleasure, connection, and raw, unapologetic desire. I'm not shrinking with age. I'm expanding into the fullest, most sensual version of myself. And if that unsettles people? Good.

I'm not short of sleazy men sliding into my DMs. It's like once you hit 50 and still look half-decent in a bikini, the internet opens its gates and lets the creeps flood in. My boundaries haven't slipped. I usually block and move on without a second thought. But one young man, and I use "man" loosely, managed to catch my attention.

Over the course of eight months, he messaged me, got blocked, created new profiles, and messaged again. Rinse and repeat. I told him, clearly and firmly, that I wasn't interested. He was far too young, barely in his 30s, which for me just feels off. Like dating someone who doesn't remember dial-up internet. But his sheer persistence started to amuse me. He wasn't giving up.

One day he messaged, "I'll pay you £1000 just to meet you."

I replied, half-joking, "Make it five."

He shot back instantly: "Will you have sex with me for that?"

I did not. But I'd be lying if I said I didn't laugh or even think about it. I'm still thinking about it. I mean, is it really prostitution when half the internet is selling tit pics for the price of a coffee on OnlyFans? At least this guy is being direct about the transaction. Most recently, he upped his offer to ten grand. Ten. *Thousand.* And I'd be lying if I said I wasn't tempted. It's not like I haven't fucked anyone for free and they certainly didn't come with luxury perks. There's a part of me that finds his persistence flattering, and another part that's just intrigued by the audacity of it all. Would I do it? Probably not. But the fact I get to even *consider* it at this age, on my terms is a delicious little reminder of the power that comes with truly owning your sexuality. Such audacity is tragic and funny. And if nothing else, it proves the power shift that happens when you hit midlife, step into your worth, and stop chasing because suddenly, you become the one being chased.

Women in their 50s are more sexually loose than society likes to admit. We're making up for lost time with a fierce hunger and unapologetic freedom. For me, that hunger didn't even begin to roar until midlife. I went from a long-term relationship at 17 that lasted seven years straight into a marriage at 25. I could count the number of men I'd slept with on one hand. But now? I can't even keep track, and that number didn't start rising until I reclaimed my life and my body in midlife. It's like the years of restraint, duty, and playing by the rules were just the warm-up act. Now, the main show is all about pleasure, exploration, and owning every inch of who I am. I am not a slut. I am a woman in tune with her sexuality. I am confident, curious, and unapologetic. There's a world of difference, and it's high time we stop confusing boldness with shame. Having sex is normal. I am fiercely against slut-shaming. It's a label given to us by a misogynist society aimed to make us feel bad and it is one of the cruelest ways women are taught to police themselves from the moment they start figuring out who they are. Society wants us to feel shame for owning our bodies and desires, to tuck ourselves away quietly and apologize for wanting pleasure. I refuse to buy into that bullshit. Being in tune with my sexuality isn't a flaw or a failure, it's a rebellion, a celebration, and ultimately, a form of self-respect.

Ironically, I've been celibate for 18 months now as I choose quality over quantity. Freedom is not just saying yes. Sometimes it's about knowing when to say no.

I have loved, I have lost, and I have discarded. Sometimes with a smile, sometimes with a sigh. But I still hold hope that my ideal man will come charging into my life one day. Not to rescue me, because I'm not a damsel in distress. No, he'll come as an equal, a partner in crime, someone who sparks my fire, challenges me, and walks beside me in this wild, wonderful journey. Someone who sees me, all of me, and loves me not despite my freedom, but because of it. Honestly, I'm excited at the prospect of falling in love again. Messy, thrilling, and completely on my own terms. I am the prize.

CHAPTER EIGHT: THE POWER OF CONFIDENCE

Here's another truth no one tells you in your 20s: no one is really looking at you. And if they are, they're too wrapped up in their own insecurities to remember what shoes you wore, how many lines are around your mouth, or whether you "should" be wearing that leather jacket at your age. I'm not in competition with 25-year-olds. I don't want their life, their skin, or their chaos. Let them have it — I've done my time. Confidence in your 50s is peace. It's about power. It's about dressing how you want, speaking your mind, and walking into every room like you belong there — because you *do*.

And guess what? The moment you stop trying to fit in is the moment you stand out.

The delicious freedom of your 50s? You finally realise that. You finally stop giving a fuck. Confidence in your 50s isn't loud or attention-seeking. It's not about proving anything. It's about ease. It's about walking into a room without shrinking, not because you think you're the hottest person there, but because you no longer care if you are. You don't need permission to take up space. You just do. When you hit your 50s, you've done the time. You've survived heartbreaks, careers, chaos, children (or not), marriages (or not), disappointments, celebrations, surgeries, stretch marks, and at least one deeply regrettable haircut. You've lived. So why on earth would the opinions of strangers — or even people you know — hold more weight than your own? Confidence is no longer something I try on like an outfit. It's something I wear under my skin, behind my eyes, in the way I carry myself. It's the lift in my chin. The unapologetic way I say, "Actually, I'll do it *my* way."

This is the decade where you shed the heavy coat of "Should."
I *should* look younger.
I *should* be more successful
I should cover up my cleavage.
Fuck that. Who made up those rules? The same people who think women over 40 shouldn't have long hair or wear skirts above the knee. Hell, mine just skim over my arse cheeks.
By the time you reach 50 you should be living life outside society's expectations of you which is incredibly freeing and empowering. When I

was 29 I felt the urge to have a baby before I was 30 as that was expected of me. Before I had kids, I would travel to far flung destinations on a whim. When my first boyfriend and I split up, I booked a return flight to Sydney and explored the Gold Coast of Australia alone. The following year I went to Bali and Japan. While most people would indulge in retail therapy when they were feeling down, I perked up by booking a flight to a destination I had never been to. When I had an argument with my ex husband before we were married, I booked a flight to New York and turned up at the airport with my handbag, passport, toothbrush and some spare underwear. I was so furious I just wanted to get on a flight and disappear for a week. I returned a week later with a suitcase stuffed with a lavish new wardrobe and a credit card thoroughly indulged. When my kids came along I felt I was shrinking. Naturally my needs became less of a priority as I raised them and the far flung trips became more infrequent. I am so sick of society's expectations of women. It can be brutal for your confidence. Stick two fingers up at it. Stop trying to squeeze yourself into a box that was never made for you, constantly judged no matter what you do or don't do. They want us to be perfect mothers, impeccable partners, effortless beauties, and saints who never put ourselves first. Well, I'm done playing by their rules. So here's me, sticking two fingers up at all that noise because my life, my body, and my happiness aren't up for debate or approval.

Society often defines success through career achievements, wealth, or status. But success is deeply personal. It could mean having meaningful relationships, achieving personal growth, experiencing freedom, or even just being content. Success for me is looking at my children who have grown into amazing, kind and emphatic humans. Looking at them truly makes me happy and defines success on my own terms and not by society's expectations, other people's timelines, or social media highlights. Real success is living in alignment with your values, passions, and peace of mind.

Society often pushes a "one-size-fits-all" approach to life, but your path is unique. Trust your intuition and inner wisdom to guide you. You might not always follow the conventional route, but that's okay. Believing in yourself is the first step toward living authentically.

People will always have opinions, but what matters most is how you feel about yourself. Letting go of the fear of judgment from others is freeing. It's liberating to know that you don't have to meet expectations that don't serve your happiness or purpose.

Often, society places value on certain milestones, like marriage, children, a specific career, or owning property. But you are allowed to prioritize different things whether it be travel, creative pursuits, a new hobby, self-discovery, or community-building. Don't feel the need to follow traditional life paths if they don't resonate with you.

We live in a world that values perfection especially on social media which is utter bullshit. Like most comedians who are depressed in real life, social media is a dangerous act. But the truth is, life is not lived through a beauty filter. It is unpredictable. Stop striving for perfection and start embracing who you are right now, flaws and all. And remember there is no such thinking as perfection because your perception isn't the same as another.

Instead of chasing what society says will make you happy, focus on cultivating your own happiness. You don't need external validation to feel worthy or fulfilled. Whether it's through hobbies, relationships, or personal reflection, make your happiness a priority and give yourself permission to create joy in your life.

If there's a societal norm you don't agree with, challenge it. It can be in your career, relationships, or lifestyle. Questioning the status quo can feel rebellious, but it also opens the door to a deeper, more authentic life.

Society often tells you that you need to follow a strict timeline—graduate, get a job, settle down, have children, retire. But there's no rush! Life doesn't have to be linear. Celebrate the freedom to make your own choices and go at your own pace. Don't feel the need to follow a prescribed timeline if it doesn't suit you.

When you live outside societal expectations, it's important to surround yourself with people who understand and support your journey. Find friends, mentors, and communities that value individuality and authenticity. These relationships will nurture your growth and help you stay true to yourself. I have let go of so many friendships that didn't align with me.

Life can be unpredictable, and embracing uncertainty is key to living authentically. It's okay not to have everything figured out. Embrace the unknown and let it be a part of the adventure.

Instead of focusing on meeting external expectations, think about the kind of legacy you want to leave. What impact do you want to have on the world or those around you? Live your life in a way that reflects the person you truly are and the difference you want to make.

Confidence in your 50s isn't about perfection, it's about power. The quiet, unshakable kind that comes from knowing who you are, what you've survived, and what you're no longer willing to tolerate. It's not about having all the answers, but trusting yourself to find them. After decades of living, loving, losing, and learning, your 50s offer the gift of perspective and with that, the freedom to show up boldly, speak your truth, and take up space unapologetically. Confidence at this stage isn't loud; it doesn't need to be. It's lived-in. It's earned. And it's yours to wear like armour as you step into the next chapter of your life. Fearless, focused, and finally free.

You know what boils my piss? When someone starts a sentence.. "At your age you shouldn't...."As if my age is some invisible leash holding me back from doing what I want, from wearing what I want, loving who I want, or chasing what sets my soul on fire. Newsflash: age isn't a rulebook, it's just a number. So if I want to dance on tables, as I have done multiple times, or wear a killer outfit showing off my magnificent natural breasts, or jump on a plane at midnight, I bloody well will. And anyone who tries to tell me otherwise can go fuck themselves . But let's be honest, they probably won't, because they're too uptight to even loosen up. Meanwhile, I'm out here living loud and free, and that's the real rebellion..

You should be exactly who you are, only more unapologetically and louder. Dress for you, not them.Wear the bold lip. Rock the tight jeans. Chop your hair or grow it wild. Style isn't about age. It's about attitude. If you want to wear sequins to the supermarket, do it. You've earned the right. You don't owe anyone a neutral palette and modest hemlines. I still wear a string bikini, much to the disgust of the Daily Mail but no one told them the style police retired in 1998. When you wear what makes you feel good. Whether it's a power blazer, a plunging neckline, or a velvet suit in hot pink , you radiate something that can't be bought: self-possession. That's the stuff real confidence is made of.And trust me, people notice that more than they'll ever notice your crow's feet.

There's a particular kind of power that comes with age: you've got receipts. You've been through things. You've proven to yourself, maybe quietly, maybe dramatically, that you can handle life. That kind of history gives you weight. When you speak, people listen, not because you're trying to dominate the conversation, but because you speak with the clarity of someone who has nothing to prove.

So walk into the meeting. Take the mic. Start the business. Say what you mean. Flirt shamelessly. Dance without the excuse of alcohol or a party. Order the damn dessert. You don't need to apologise or explain yourself.

In your 50s, something else extraordinary happens: you finally stop competing. You're not looking sideways at the 25-year-olds. You're not trying to play a game where the rules were never made for you. You're too busy writing your own. Confidence in your 50s is rooted in peace. I don't need to win your approval, I've already won my own.

So what if your face has changed? So what if your boobs sit a little lower or your knees creak? You are *alive,* and your body has carried you this far. That's not something to hide or fight and that's something to celebrate. Your body may have grown and birthed babies. Now that's a superpower in itself.

Confidence doesn't mean you never feel doubt. It just means you don't let doubt run the show. It's the voice in your head that says, "You've got this," when everything feels uncertain. And guess what? That voice grows louder with every decade. Make confidence your best friend. Feed it. Dress it up. Take it out. Let it speak first. Let it answer emails. Let it go on dates. Let it pick the restaurant. Let it walk into the court room, the boardroom, the dressing room. Let it steer. You've spent decades growing into who you are. The rest of your life? That's the runway. Strut like no one's watching. Because honestly, they're not and if they are, you're giving them something worth watching.

For me, confidence didn't arrive on a silver tray one morning with a motivational quote and a green smoothie. It showed up when I boarded the flight to Cyprus without a return ticket after ten years of thinking about it. That one decision, painful and messy as it was, unlocked something that had been sleeping inside me for years: a sense of ownership over my own life. It was like walking out of a cage I hadn't realised I'd been sitting in. I found my voice. I found my rhythm. And most importantly, I found *myself*. He told me I didnt need to go to the hairdresser or get my nails done. He told me botox was for sad insecure people but guess what? I did all that. I became a cliche and joined a gym, dropped 25 kilos, got hair extensions, pointy acrylic nails, false lash extensions and milligrams of botox. I loved it. I felt glamorous, gorgeous and sexy.

There's something radical about choosing yourself. Leaving a relationship, especially one that's lasted years, can feel like standing at the edge of a cliff. But here's the thing: the fall isn't as scary as staying stuck. And when you leap, when you *choose* your freedom, your peace, your future, confidence rushes in to meet you.

I grew in confidence not because everything suddenly became easy, but because I proved to myself that I could handle it. That I could rebuild. Reinvent. Reclaim. That I wasn't too old or too late or too "past it" to start again. Confidence is the best friend you take everywhere now. She whispers, *You've got this* when you're nervous. She helps you walk taller in rooms that used to intimidate you. She picks out your clothes in the morning and tells you the truth when no one else will: *You look incredible, and you don't need to justify a damn thing.*Leaving my marriage was the beginning of my second act. Not the end of love or excitement or beauty, but the rebirth of *me.*Confidence is no longer something I try on like an outfit. It's something I wear under my skin, behind my eyes, in the way I carry myself. It's the lift in my chin. The unapologetic way I say, "Actually, I'll do it *my* way."

It's my best friend now. Confidence isn't always about looking polished. Sometimes it's about standing at the edge of something that terrifies you and doing it anyway. That's what I learned when I booked a trip to Hong Kong, entirely on my own, after years of playing it safe. No one pushed me. No one held my hand. I just decided: I need to do something that reminds me I'm alive. And so I did.

I went to Disneyland. Yes, a grown woman at Disneyland Hong Kong. Alone. And I rode a rollercoaster, something I've always hated. The kind of thing I used to avoid while politely holding everyone's bags. But not this time. I stood in the queue, heart thumping, and I got on that ride. I screamed the whole way. I hated every second. And I've never felt prouder.

But that wasn't even the biggest test.I took a cable car to Ngong Ping. It's the world's tallest cable car. Let me tell you, when that glass box lifted off the ground and I saw the mountain drop away beneath my feet, I was *shit scared*. My palms were sweating, my breath shallow, my inner voice yelling *get off this thing now*. But I stayed.I sat in that swaying little glass box in the sky, completely out of my comfort zone, completely alone and something remarkable happened. I didn't die. I didn't fall. I didn't lose control even though I was shaking and sweating. I made it. I stepped out of fear and into power. When we landed, I stepped onto solid ground not just relieved but slightly more proud of myself..

Because that's the thing about stepping outside your comfort zone: you realise how small that zone really was. And how much of life is waiting just outside it. After that trip, I realised confidence doesn't come from staying comfortable. It comes from doing hard things and proving to yourself I can handle this. Whether it's a solo trip, a rollercoaster, a courtroom, or leaving a marriage, every brave step forward changes you.

And you don't go back. So ride the rollercoaster. Take the flight. Sit in the scary cable car. Let your knees shake if they need to. But go anyway. Because when it's over, you'll walk away a little braver, a little taller, and a hell of a lot more alive.

And whether you're freshly single, newly bold, or just starting to rediscover the woman you buried for years beneath expectations, know this: it's never too late. Confidence doesn't come from approval. It comes from freedom. From choosing yourself. From doing the things they said you *shouldn't* and loving every minute of it.

Get Botox if you want. I didn't get it because I was ashamed of aging. I got it because I wanted to walk out the door and feel fabulous again. And

I did. That was the point. It wasn't about reversing the years, it was about celebrating the woman I've become. Wear the lashes. Rock the bikini, or fuck it, go topless. Reclaim your damn sparkle. No one's watching and if they are, let them wonder how you got so fierce.

Confidence is often seen as a mysterious quality, something only a few people seem to possess in abundance. But here's the truth: confidence is not something you're born with; it's something you can cultivate. And once you do, it has the power to transform every area of your life: Your career, your relationships, your self-image, and even your sense of purpose.

Confidence can radically shift your mindset, open new opportunities, and lead to a life filled with possibility. Confidence isn't about being perfect or never doubting yourself. It's about trusting in your own abilities, knowing your worth, and taking action despite fear. The more you believe in yourself, the more you can achieve, and the more your life will change in ways you never imagined.

Confidence is like a ripple in water. It spreads, influencing everything around you. When you exude confidence, people respond to you differently. You carry yourself with a quiet assurance that makes others take notice. Opportunities come your way, doors open, and situations that once felt intimidating start to feel more manageable.

But more than how others perceive you, confidence changes how you perceive yourself. When you believe in your abilities, you're more likely to take risks, try new things, and step outside of your comfort zone. The truth is, confidence is key to unlocking doors. Doors to personal growth, career advancement, stronger relationships, and a more fulfilling life.

The first tangible way confidence can change your life is through the willingness to take risks. Without confidence, we often hold ourselves back, fearing failure or rejection. But when you truly believe in yourself, you understand that failure is not the end of the world, it's part of the journey. It's a learning experience, not a reflection of your worth.

A confident mindset allows you to take risks because you trust that, no matter the outcome, you will grow from the experience. You stop waiting for the "perfect moment" and begin creating opportunities for yourself. Whether it's applying for your dream job, starting a new business, or speaking up in a meeting, confidence gives you the courage to act.

At the heart of confidence is the ability to quiet your inner critic, the voice that tells you you're not good enough, not smart enough, or not capable enough. We all have moments of self-doubt, but when you choose to challenge these negative beliefs, you reclaim your power.

Confidence doesn't mean that you never feel unsure, it means that you acknowledge those doubts and continue to move forward anyway. It's about choosing to believe in your abilities and taking action despite the voice of doubt.

When you confront limiting beliefs head-on, you begin to break free from the patterns that have held you back. You start replacing "I can't" with "I can" and "I'm not good enough" with "I am enough, just as I am." Over time, these shifts in mindset begin to feel natural, and you find yourself taking bolder actions and achieving things you once thought were impossible.

One of the strongest aspects of confidence is its ability to build resilience. Life is full of ups and downs, and there will always be challenges, setbacks, and moments of doubt. But a confident person views these obstacles not as roadblocks but as opportunities for growth.

When you trust yourself, you trust that you have the inner strength to handle whatever comes your way. You don't see failure as the end, you see it as part of the process. This mindset allows you to bounce back faster and stronger after difficult times. You develop a sense of inner security, knowing that no matter what happens, you can navigate through it and come out the other side wiser and more capable. At the time of writing this book I am two weeks away from a court case in Cyprus where I am suing the bank for misselling me a mortgage that could see me lose my home. I don't know what the future is going to be, I don't know where I am going to live but I am going to trust the process. I have been a badass for suing a major bank in Cyprus. I am not going down without a fight. And my identity is not defined by bricks, my home is within myself. No matter what happens, I will handle it.

Confidence doesn't just affect your career or personal goal. It profoundly impacts your relationships with others. When you believe in your own worth, you set boundaries, communicate your needs, and foster connections based on mutual respect and understanding. You stop seeking validation from others and start choosing relationships that uplift and support you.

When you're confident in who you are, you attract people who value and appreciate you for your authentic self. You stop wasting time in relationships that drain you or make you feel less than. Confidence allows you to say no when necessary and yes to the relationships that truly nourish you.

Confidence also helps you become a better communicator. When you believe in your ideas and opinions, you're able to express them more clearly and assertively, which fosters more meaningful and honest conversations. Whether it's with a partner, a friend, or a colleague, confidence helps you show up as your most authentic self.

Perhaps the deepest way confidence can change your life is by shifting how you see yourself. When you believe in yourself, your self-esteem grows. You begin to recognize your worth, not based on external accomplishments or the approval of others, but based on the fact that you are inherently valuable as you are.

A confident woman knows her strengths and accepts her flaws. She doesn't measure her worth by comparison to others or by society's standards of perfection. She understands that her uniqueness is what makes her powerful. And this deep, unshakeable sense of self-love creates a foundation for everything else to flourish.

Confidence helps you become comfortable in your own skin, embrace your individuality, and fully appreciate who you are. You begin to take care of yourself, not because you feel you have to, but because you recognize you are deserving of that care and attention.

Confidence is not a destination. It's a practice. It's something you build every single day. But once you begin to cultivate it, you'll notice shifts happening in every area of your life. The more confident you become, the more you'll realize that you are capable of achieving anything you set your mind to.

Believe in yourself. Trust that you have the strength, wisdom and resilience to overcome any challenge that comes your way. Know that your worth is not dependent on the approval of others, but is inherent in who you are.

Step into your power. Let your confidence radiate from within, and watch as your life transforms before your eyes. When you believe in yourself, you open the door to a future full of possibilities, and you begin living the life you've always dreamed of.

Believe in yourself. You've got this.

CHAPTER NINE; FEMINISM AND SPEAKING UP

Feminism at 50 is about owning every scar, every choice, and every damn triumph that got you here. It's about tearing down the outdated rules that tell us our worth fades with age or that we should quietly step back and fade out. At 50, feminism means fighting for the freedom to live fiercely, love boldly, and demand respect, not just for the young and shiny, but for every woman who refuses to be sidelined by society's narrow definition of relevance.

Speaking up in your 50s is more than an act of feminism. It is an act of self-respect, legacy, and liberation. At this stage of life, our voice carries the weight of lived experience. Choosing to use it disrupts the outdated notion that older women should shrink, stay quiet, or fade into the background. Speaking up isn't just about challenging sexism or ageism, it's about modelling courage for the next generation, standing in your truth, and refusing to let anyone else write your narrative. It's reclaiming space, setting boundaries, and making it clear that your worth doesn't expire with age. Every time you speak up, you remind the world and yourself that your story still matters.

For too long, women have been taught to keep quiet, to stay small, and to avoid rocking the boat. From a young age, many of us are socialized to be agreeable, to smile and nod, to keep the peace, and to avoid confrontation. These lessons are deeply ingrained in our society, often making us hesitate to speak up when something feels wrong or unjust.

However, one of the most empowering acts of feminism is the willingness to raise our voices when needed. And we should do it more than ever, especially as in some countries such as Afghanistan women aren't even allowed to look out of the window. Speaking up doesn't always mean giving a speech or standing on a podium. It can be as simple as calling out inappropriate behavior, asserting your rights in the workplace, or expressing your opinion in a conversation.

Your voice is powerful, and when you speak out, you send a message: "*I matter. My opinions and experiences matter. And I deserve to be heard.*"

When women speak up, we are not just advocating for ourselves—we are also advocating for every woman who has been silenced, every girl who is told her voice doesn't count, and every person who has ever been denied equality. Speaking up is an act of solidarity, a way of showing that we are all in this fight for equality together.

Despite the importance of speaking, many of us are afraid to do so. Fear of judgment, fear of being labeled difficult or emotional, and fear of retaliation are common reasons why women often silence themselves. Fear of disrupting the status quo or losing relationships. Whether personal or professional, it can make us shrink back into silence but don't allow that to happen.

The fear of speaking up is often the very thing that holds us back from experiencing real growth and change. We are told that voicing our opinion can make us unpopular, but in reality, speaking up is often the very thing that inspires others to do the same. Change begins with someone's courage to speak up, and that someone can be you. I have done it hundreds of times and I get messages all the time from women thanking me for my boldness. But it's just me being me. I won't be silenced. As a mother it's my responsibility to be vocal, to ensure my children grow up in a world where equality isn't just an ideal, but a reality. Feminism isn't about hating men or burning the bra. It's about demanding fairness, dignity, and the freedom to exist fully and unapologetically. If my voice shakes the status quo, then so be it. I'd rather be too loud than complicit.

It's important to acknowledge that fear is natural. You're not alone in feeling nervous or uncertain about using your voice. But what matters is recognizing that fear doesn't have to stop you. The more you practice using your voice, the more confident you will become in standing up for yourself, and the more you'll see how much your words matter.

Speaking up doesn't need to be dramatic or confrontational. It can start with small, everyday actions, and gradually grow into more powerful moments of advocacy.

The first step in using your voice is finding opportunities to speak up in everyday situations. Whether it's in a group discussion at work, during a family conversation, or among friends, don't be afraid to share your opinion.

If someone makes a sexist remark, a joke about women, or undermines your abilities, it's important to respond. You don't have to be confrontational; simply saying something like, *"I don't think that's funny,"* or *"That comment doesn't sit right with me,"* can make a huge difference. Small moments like these show that you won't tolerate injustice and that you're willing to stand firm in your beliefs.

Setting boundaries is a powerful form of speaking up. Feminism teaches us that we are entitled to space, respect, and fairness. Speaking up for yourself is an act of self-love and empowerment.

In situations where you feel disrespected, don't be afraid to assert your boundaries. Whether it's in a workplace setting or with family members, clearly state what you're willing to accept and what you're not. When you speak up for yourself, you create a space for others to respect your needs and desires.

Feminism isn't just about lifting yourself up, it's about lifting others. One of the most powerful ways to use your voice is by advocating for other women. If you witness someone being treated unfairly, whether it's a colleague being passed over for a promotion or a friend being gaslit in a relationship, speak up on their behalf.

You might say something like, *"I don't think that's fair to her,"* or *"This behavior is unacceptable."* Using your voice to advocate for other women amplifies the collective power of the feminist movement and shows solidarity in the fight for gender equality.

Feminism calls for the courage to speak out on issues that matter to you, even when it feels uncomfortable. Whether it's advocating for reproductive rights, gender equality in the workplace, or justice for victims of abuse, your voice can make a difference in pushing for social change.

Don't underestimate the impact of your words. Every conversation you have about gender equality, every stance you take on social justice issues, contributes to the larger movement for change. It may not always feel like a big deal, but when women stand together and use their voices, they create a collective force that cannot be ignored. I am regularly posting reels on social media ranting about things that have happened that I feel have been unjust. Mostly around the way the teachers talk to my children in school.

It's easy to worry that you'll say the wrong thing or make a mistake when speaking up. But feminism isn't about perfection; it's about progress. It's about learning, growing, and doing better each day. Don't let fear of mistakes silence you. Every time you speak, you learn and evolve. If you do make a mistake, it's okay. Apologize, learn from it, and keep going. What matters is that you keep showing up for yourself and for others.

Every time you speak up, you create a ripple effect. Your words have the potential to inspire others to use their voices, to create a wave of change that can grow into something powerful and unstoppable. Feminism is built on the voices of women who are brave enough to speak up, even when it's difficult or scary.

Remember, the act of speaking up doesn't just change the immediate situation, it shifts the culture. It challenges long-standing systems of inequality. It changes how we view ourselves and each other. By speaking up, you are contributing to a world where women are no longer silenced, dismissed, or invisible.

Feminism and speaking up go hand-in-hand. Feminism is about equality, justice, and respect and the best way to advocate for these values is by using your voice. Every time you speak up, you challenge the status quo and stand in your power. It is an act of love, not only for yourself but for every woman who has been silenced, ignored, or denied her rights.

Finding your voice is not easy, but it is essential. The world needs your voice—your perspective, your insights, and your experience. Don't let fear or doubt hold you back. The more you speak up, the more you will inspire others to do the same. Together, we can create a world where women are no longer afraid to speak their truths, stand up for what is right, and fight for a future of equality and justice. When we speak up, we change the world.

Feminism is often misunderstood, misrepresented, and, unfortunately, even vilified. One of the most pervasive myths about feminism is that it's about hating men or rejecting them entirely. But the truth couldn't be farther from that. Feminism isn't about "man-hating"; it's about advocating for equality, respect, and fairness for everyone.

The reality is that as women, we are tired of the societal conditioning that has made us feel that we have to settle for relationships, friendships, or partnerships with men who don't contribute positively to our lives. Feminism calls for us to hold ourselves to a higher standard, to demand respect, and to focus on relationships that are mutually beneficial, whether romantic or platonic.

Feminism pushes us to redefine what we deserve and to hold ourselves to higher standards, not because we think we're superior to others, but because we understand our own worth. For far too long, women have been socialized to settle for less, to accept unhealthy relationships, to tolerate disrespect, or to believe that our needs are secondary to others. Feminism says, *enough*.

Having high standards doesn't make you demanding or unrealistic. It makes you self-respecting. Feminism teaches us to ask for what we need, not to apologize for it. It teaches us to refuse to settle for relationships that diminish our sense of self-worth. If you're constantly giving more than you're receiving, constantly accommodating someone else's needs while ignoring your own, then you're not in a healthy relationship. You're in an imbalance. And feminism is all about equality.

This doesn't mean rejecting men entirely. It means rejecting men who don't treat you as an equal or who don't bring anything positive into your life. Feminism empowers us to choose the kind of people we want to spend our time with. It encourages us to stop feeling guilty for walking away from relationships that aren't serving us.

The most common misconception about feminism is that it's an anti-man movement. But feminism is about advocating fairness, respect and equality for all genders. It's about creating a world where women have the same opportunities, respect, and choices as men. It's about understanding that our value isn't tied to the approval of others, including men.

When women demand respect in relationships or choose not to settle for less, it's not a rejection of men. It's a rejection of *poor treatment*. It's about knowing your worth and choosing relationships that honor that. It's not about excluding men; it's about including the right men.

If we choose not to stay in relationships that don't add value to our lives, we're not "man-haters." We're women who know our worth and refuse to accept anything less than what we deserve. This is not about gender, it's about humanity. It's about the basic right to be treated with respect, kindness, and love, without having to fight for it.

Feminism does not demand a world without men. It calls for a world where women's voices are heard, respected, and valued equally. It calls for all relationships whether romantic, platonic, or professional that are based on mutual respect, support, and growth.

We aren't "man-haters" because we demand value. We simply recognize that our time, energy, and love should be given to those who honor and contribute to our lives in positive ways. Feminism teaches us that we deserve relationships that bring out the best in us, relationships that make us feel heard, respected, and empowered.

At 50 I feel I am just stepping into my power and I am not prepared to grow older quietly. At 50, feminism means turning up the volume, breaking the silence, and smashing the glass ceilings that try to cage us in invisibility. I demand to be seen, heard, and be celebrated for my strength, my stories, and my unapologetic power. Feminism at 50 is fierce, unapologetic, and deeply rooted in life experience. It's about fighting not just for your own seat at the table, but for your daughters, your granddaughters, and every woman who's still being told to shrink herself. At 50, you don't ask permission. You speak, you act, and you stand in your strength.

CHAPTER TEN: SOLO TRAVEL

There's something quietly radical about a woman in her 50s booking a one-way ticket, packing a bag, and setting off on her own. Not for work. Not for family. But just for herself. To go to the places she's dreamed about while sitting at desks, changing nappies, or putting everyone else's needs first. Solo travel at this stage of life isn't just a holiday, it's a reclamation. It's your passport to freedom.

When you're younger, solo travel can be about finding yourself. In my 20s I went to Bali, Japan, Los Angeles and Palm Springs on my own. But in your 50s, solo travel hits differently. It's not about escape, it's about expansion. It's about honouring the self you've already found. You don't need to prove anything. You don't have to compromise on where you go, what you do, or who you go with because this time, it's all about what lights you up. Whether it's wandering through the souks of Marrakech, sipping wine on a Tuscan terrace, hiking the Camino de Santiago, or simply sitting by the sea in Greece with a good book and no agenda, you get to choose.

There's a certain confidence that comes with age that makes solo travel feel not just possible, but powerful. You've handled chaos, raised families, navigated relationships, survived heartbreak, burnout, and maybe even menopause. Booking a train in a foreign language or getting lost in a city isn't intimidating. It's an adventure. You no longer apologise for asking for directions, changing your mind, or ordering dessert for one. As women, we've often been told that it's "brave" to travel alone, especially as we get older. And in fact the fastest-growing group of solo travellers is aged over 50, with many citing a desire for freedom, self-discovery, or a second chance in life.

Of course you could just stay at home . Stay stuck in the familiar out of fear, to keep waiting for the right time or the "ight person to come with you. That's the real risk, waiting so long you forget what it is you actually wanted. Because here's the truth: life is too short to keep postponing your joy.That dream trip you've had pinned on your vision board for twenty years? Go. That place that tugs at your soul every time you see it in a film or a magazine? Book it. Don't worry if you don't speak the language. Don't worry if it's not practical. Don't worry if someone tells you it's selfish or indulgent. You've spent your life being responsible. Now it's time to be a little rebellious.Solo travel doesn't have to mean a round-the-world trip. It can be a weekend away in the countryside, a spa break alone, or just a few days in a city you've never explored. It's not about the distance, it's about the decision. The decision to go. To step into your power. To write your own story. To remind yourself that your life is still unfolding. For me, the shift began when I moved to Cyprus alone. Uprooting my life wasn't easy, but it was the beginning of something transformative. In the quiet moments under the sun, surrounded by a new rhythm and a language I didn't speak fluently, I remembered who I was. It was the first time I'd truly listened to myself in years. No distractions. No noise. Just me, my thoughts, and the promise of something more. That move cracked something open.

My trip to Hong Kong was booked on a whim with three weeks' notice to myself after I won a new PR client and spent their booking invoice on myself. No agenda, no one to consult, no reason other than because I wanted to. That trip was a turning point. I wandered the city streets, took ferries, ate alone in rooftop restaurants, and felt more alive than I had in years. It wasn't about ticking off tourist sites. It was about reclaiming freedom. It was about reminding myself that I didn't need permission to explore or experience wonder. I only needed my passport and the courage to say yes to myself.

To be honest travelling alone has never felt scary for me it feels like a reward. I have been on countless press trips to Europe on my own and even went to Palm Springs for a job interview.

My flight was overbooked and it was Boxing Day in 1994, an era before mobile phones. I was supposed to be met at Los Angeles airport by the people from ABC TV in Palm Springs for the interview and they were ferrying my back to my hotel. But I was bumped onto a flight five hours later and landed after midnight. With no one to meet me I found a car rental and drive myself to Palm Springs. Having never driven in America and relying on a paper road map, let's just say it was an adventure. But I made it to the hotel I knew I was booked into and I was super proud of myself. That journey, though simple on the surface, marked a turning point. It was proof that I could rely on myself, trust my instincts, and navigate the unknown alone. Solo travel is the best. You don't have to negotiate plans, share the bathroom, or wait for anyone else to want the same things. You wake up and choose what you eat, where you go, how long you stay. It's your journey, entirely on your terms. I love it. And here's the thing: life is too short to wait. Waiting for the perfect time. Waiting for a partner. Waiting for retirement. The truth is, the perfect moment rarely arrives tied up in a bow. Sometimes you just have to go. Book the ticket. Take the risk. Let the world surprise you.

Whether it's a week in Hong Kong, a new life in Cyprus, or a spontaneous escape to somewhere that's been calling you for years. Not because you're lost, but because you're finally free to find more.

When I first got with my ex husband, he hated going on holiday and had to be coerced into it. For weeks I asked him to book the same week off so we could plan a trip and when it came to it he made excuse after excuse not to go. In the end I left him painting the bathroom while I booked a flight to New York and just went with a credit card, a hand bag, toothbrush and a change of underwear. I planned to buy everything I needed there and I did. I am never waiting for anyone.

Honestly, I don't understand why more people don't travel solo. I hear so many excuses. Too old, too tired, too broke, too afraid. But you don't have to fly across the world to feel the shift. Start small. Book a night in a beautiful hotel in your own city. Get a room with crisp white sheets, fluffy towels, and a view of something that isn't your daily routine. Sit in the bar alone and order something that feels like a celebration. Even just one night away can change your mindset, shake off the dust, and remind you that you're still a woman who deserves pleasure, quiet, and newness.

Travel doesn't have to be expensive or extravagant, it just has to be *yours*. You've spent decades meeting everyone else's needs. Isn't it time to meet your own? And I drained my bank account to go to Hong Kong, a month before Christmas. And of course, there's *always* something else to spend the money on. A bill, a broken boiler, someone's emergency. For years, I did what so many women do. I paid the bills, put everyone else first, made do. I told myself I'd travel "one day," once things were more stable, once there was more time, once everyone else had what they needed. But one day never comes unless you make it.

I'd spent a lifetime putting myself at the bottom of the list. So I made a decision. **No more**. Me first. Not in a selfish way, but in a *necessary* one. Because if I didn't start choosing myself, no one else was going to do it for me. That trip to Hong Kong? That wasn't reckless, it was overdue. It was me claiming joy, claiming space, claiming my right to explore and experience the world on my own terms.

You don't have to justify wanting more. You don't have to explain why you crave adventure, solitude, or a break from the roles you've played for decades. Wanting to travel is reason enough. And choosing to finally invest in yourself, whether it's a plane ticket or a posh hotel room for one night, isn't indulgent. It's a form of healing. Of rebellion. Of radical self-respect. Because the woman who boards a plane alone in her 50s isn't running away. She's returning to herself

You don't have to fly across the world to feel the shift. Start small. Book a night in a beautiful hotel in your own city. Get a room with crisp white sheets, fluffy towels, and a view of something that isn't your daily routine. Sit in the bar alone and order something that feels like a celebration. Take a train to a new town, walk the streets with no agenda, sit in a café with your journal. Even just one night away can change your mindset, shake off the dust, and remind you that you're still a woman who deserves pleasure, quiet, and newness.

You'll realise how capable you are. How resourceful. How interesting. You'll strike up conversations with strangers, or not. You'll sit with your own thoughts and realise you're actually good company. You'll learn to trust your gut again, to follow your instincts, to say *yes* to that boat trip, or *no* to that guided tour. No compromises, no negotiations, just pure, unapologetic freedom.

And the best part? You'll come home changed. More certain of who you are. Less willing to shrink. Less tolerant of anything that doesn't serve you. Travel stretches you and at this stage in life, stretching isn't about discomfort. It's about expansion.

And while we're on the subject, yes, go to the bar on your own. Go clubbing on your own. Sit in a restaurant alone and order the steak and the wine and the damn dessert. Not because you're lonely, but because you're liberated. I've done it all, danced solo on a packed floor, sipped cocktails at rooftop bars with no one but the city lights for company and let me tell you, it's *brilliant*. People might stare. Let them. Most of the time, they're not judging, they're **jealous**. Jealous they don't have the guts to do what you're doing. Jealous they're still waiting for permission, still waiting for company, still worried about what people might think. But you? You're *done* with that. You've earned your freedom, and you know how to enjoy it.

There's something magnetic about a woman who does her own thing with confidence. It's not about needing attention. It's about owning your space. You become the woman others wish they could be: unapologetic, self-contained, and unbothered.The freedom you feel when you stop giving a damn what people think? That's what empowerment really looks like

CHAPTER ELEVEN: FINANCIAL FUCK UPS

I've never been good with money and if truth be told, I am still learning. There. I said it. Not because I was lazy or stupid but because no one ever taught me how to *be* good with money. I grew up in the 80s, in an era of shoulder pads, Dynasty, and buy-now-pay-later thinking. Credit was glamourised. Overspending was normal. Saving? That was for boring people. Success was measured by how many store cards you had and whether your handbag had a designer logo. I was raised on the gospel of consumption. And the message was clear: you can have it now even if you can't afford it.

I bought the handbags. The clothes. The makeup. I stacked my credit card with trips to Australia and Bali. I knew how to look like I had it together, even when I was drowning in overdraft fees and pretending the letters from the bank didn't exist.

And if I'm honest? Some of it made me feel powerful. Like I was *someone*. That dopamine hit from buying something new? It was addictive especially when so much of my life felt out of control.

But behind the glossy exterior was, and probably still is, chaos.

I didn't budget. I didn't save.

I didn't think beyond the next payday and when I got divorced, the financial reality of my life hit like a train. No backup plan. No rainy-day fund. Just bills, debt, and a very expensive education in financial wake-up calls.

I left home at 18 because I had no choice. While my friends were living rent-free, saving their wages or blowing them on weekend trips and designer drugs, I was paying rent, bills, council tax, the lot. I didn't have a fallback. I *was* the fallback. And yet I was ambitious.

I got good jobs in the media, worked hard, earned decent money, and when the industry started chewing people up and spitting them out, I got made redundant more than once. Each time came with a decent payoff, and each time I tried to be smart with it.

I invested in property. And for a while, it worked. There were moments where it looked like I'd made it. Like the financial pressure was easing and I could breathe. I was a landlord with multiple properties at one time. But life, as always, had other plans. I put a deposit down on an office block that went into liquidation as the property markets crashed. I invested in a property abroad and was missold a mortgage that sent my repayments spiraling upwards to the point that I am currently suing the bank and fighting a repossession. A tenant was murdered in one of my houses and I sold it.Deals went sideways. The cost of living kept rising.

And still no one had ever taught me how to make money *work* for me. Only how to make it *look like* I was doing well.

No one talks about the shame of not being good with money. Especially not women in midlife. We're supposed to have it all sorted by now, right? But I'll say it. I've made bad decisions. I've ignored red flags. I've made bad investments and I've spent to impress people who didn't care. I've tied my self-worth to what was in my wardrobe instead of what was in my savings account. And for a long time, I felt like a failure because of it.

Here's what changed: I stopped buying shit and lying to myself. Now my wardrobe is more Temu than Tommy Hillfiger. And I get excited by my daughters' hand me downs.

I started looking at my bank account. I made a budget. I asked for help, not from a man, but from books, podcasts, women who had *been there* and came out the other side.

I forgave myself for not knowing better. And then I decided to *do better*.

I stopped spending to numb myself.
I set boundaries around money, especially in relationships.
I learned that saying "I can't afford that right now" is not weakness, it's power.

I have never believed a man would rescue me financially. I spent 25 years in a marriage paying the mortgage and utility bills in full. I never had handouts from parents and I won't inherit anything. I have earned in excess of a million pounds but raising 6 children to adults isn't cheap and my bank balance is pathetic. Even now every spare penny I have goes on them. But I have been kinder to myself and learnt that I was never bad with money. I was doing my best with zero guidance and a ton of pressure.

Paying rent at 18 while working full-time taught me resilience most people don't learn until life slaps them later.

Being made redundant taught me that nothing is guaranteed, and everything you earn must have a plan.

Property was a good move until it wasn't. And I'm proud that I *tried*.

I don't regret my mistakes, they were my education. Expensive? Yes. But invaluable.

Most importantly...Financial freedom isn't about being rich. It's about being fearless.

Being my own provider is hard and humbling but the freedom that comes from knowing I can take care of myself and *that* is priceless. It is never too late to take control of your finances. Whether you're 35, 50, or 65 you can start today

Life is unpredictable, painful and expensive. But I have a resilient soul and you need to hear this. Right now, I haven't got much money. I don't even own a car. I'm not sitting on a pile of savings. I'm not shopping in the mall on the weekends. Some days, I'm counting pennies and living off crackers and protein shakes. Some nights, I lie awake doing mental gymnastics about bills and bank balances.But here's what I know: I'm going to be OK.

Because everything has to come crashing down sometimes, not to punish you, but to rebuild you. Stronger. Clearer. Smarter. It's not rock bottom. It's a reset.

I look at two of my closest friends, both in their 60s now. A decade ago, they were where I am: broke, broken-hearted, starting again when the world said they should be winding down. And now? They're flying. One remarried. Another bought her flat. They're thriving not because it was easy, but because they *kept going*.

So when I feel the panic rise, I remind myself:
This is just the middle of the story. Not the end. I'm not done yet. Not by a long shot.

And when it turns around, when the money comes in, when the doors open, when I look back on this chapter ,I'll say, "This is where I built my power."

Because 53 is not too late. Rock bottom is not the end. And I am not finished.

Maybe your bank account is empty. Maybe your heart is bruised. Maybe you're tired of starting over. Maybe you're wondering if it's too late to become the woman you were always meant to be. Let me tell you something: It's not too late. It's never too late. Like the line from the Hamilton musical, "Why do you write like you're running out of time?" trust me, you still have time.

Right now, I don't have money in the bank. I'm restructuring. There are moments I feel overwhelmed, moments I wonder if I've made all the wrong turns.

But deep down, I believe: I'm going to be OK.

Everything crashing down?

That's the rebuild. That's the foundation for what's next.

I've seen it happen with my own friends; women in their 60s who were skint and starting over at 50, and now they're soaring.

So I hold onto that truth. I hold onto the belief that this isn't the end. This is the beginning.

And through it all, there's this:

Thank God my children are OK.

They live at home, they've saved thousands from their wages, and they've got a financial head-start that I never had. That's not luck, that's *me*. That's me making sure they don't repeat the same patterns. That's a mother breaking cycles, even while struggling quietly behind the scenes.

So yes, some good has come from it. A lot of good, actually. If this book teaches you anything, let it be this, You are allowed to begin again at any age. And you are never too old to change, dream, walk away from what no longer serves you. You don't have to be rich to be valuable. And you don't have to be perfect to be powerful.

Most important of all, you don't have to have it all figured out to take the next step.

You're going to die anyway so do it anyway. Live. Risk. Try. Fail. Rebuild. Laugh. Cry. Because your story isn't over, not by a long shot. And neither is mine.

CHAPTER TWELVE: PERSONAL GROWTH AND NEW OPPORTUNITIES

Turning 50 can feel like entering a new chapter of life. A chapter that comes with both a sense of accomplishment and a certain level of self-awareness. It's a time where you've lived through a lot of experiences, learned from your mistakes, and gained invaluable wisdom. But it's also a time for reinvention and embracing new opportunities.

Don't think for one moment that you're slowing down. My 50s are the perfect time to hit the reset button and explore new possibilities. I embraced passion when I hit 50. Totally unexpected, wild and physically satisfying but it didn't last but that's not the point. It woke something up in me. This was an electrifying start to my 50s, where I realised that actually, I was alive and sexy, assertive and more confident than I realised. I stepped into valid self-assurance, and owning who I am. Iif you approaching the big five o with intrepidation, shut the fuck up. This is a time to shed old limitations, challenge outdated beliefs, and pursue the things that truly light you up. Which, if you're lucky, might possibly be a younger lover. There's something incredibly powerful about a woman who knows her worth, isn't afraid to take up space, and moves through the world with a mix of sensuality and self-respect , can be one of the most powerful times in your life for personal growth. So embrace it.

Fifty is all about embracing the possibilities that come with personal growth and new opportunities in your 50s. It's a time to push past self-doubt, reclaim your sexy power, and open yourself up to the exciting chapters that lie ahead.

Don't like who you are? Reinvent yourself. By now you've likely spent decades establishing who you are whether that's as a mother, a partner, a professional, or a community member. But as you enter this new phase of life, there is a profound sense of freedom. You've learned a lot, and with that knowledge comes the ability to reinvent yourself. You are no longer tethered to the expectations and pressures of others, and you're free to design your life on your own terms.

This freedom can feel exhilarating. You have more time, more space, and more self-awareness to focus on what truly matters to you. The burdens of youth, like trying to "prove" yourself or meet external standards, begin to fall away. Instead, you can focus on the things that bring you joy, fulfillment, and a sense of purpose.

Reinvention doesn't mean abandoning who you are. It means evolving, growing, and expanding into new directions. Whether it's a new career, a new hobby, or a new relationship, or simply a physical transformation as I did, now is the time to reimagine what's possible for yourself.

Personal growth in your 50s often involves letting go of old beliefs, habits, and even relationships that no longer serve you. Over the years, you've likely accumulated ideas, stories, and patterns about who you are and what you're capable of. However, this phase of life often requires you to release some of those old ideas and make space for new, empowering ones.

Letting go can be challenging, especially if you've held onto certain beliefs or relationships for years. But the truth is, personal growth comes when you're willing to release what no longer aligns with who you are becoming. Whether it's the fear of starting something new, the comfort of old habits, or the weight of past regrets, you must be willing to let go in order to grow.

Embrace this phase, think about the things that have held you back in the past. Do you have limiting beliefs about your age or abilities? Have you been afraid to take risks or try something new because of previous failures? Embrace the limitless potential of the present moment. In your 50s, we've earned the right to create a life that feels authentic and fulfilling.

Now is a time to reexamine your career. For some, this may mean making a bold career shift or exploring new professional interests. For others, it might be about stepping back and finding new ways to contribute or giving yourself permission to slow down and focus on passions that were previously sidelined. I really hate doing what I am doing. I love writing a magazine as that's my passion, but I loathe the hustle of selling advertising, the exhausting pressure, practically begging people to work with me. I hate the fact that AI is killing my business, everyone nowadays is a self taught PR expert which leaves me where? I wondering where that puts me with decades of real experience.I haven't a clue but I am on the lookout for new opportunities but I am open to exploring new avenues. I am open to new opportunities, open to reinvention, and open to exploring paths I might never have considered before. Because giving up isn't an option but evolving is.

There's a misconception that by the time you're in your 50s, you should be winding down your career or preparing for retirement. But your 50s can be a time to step into new professional opportunities—ones that align more closely with your passions, values, and desires. Life is far from over and if you've ever dreamed of doing something different, your 50s might be the perfect time to make that leap. Whether you've always wanted to start a business, become a consultant, or explore a new industry, this is the time to take that step. You've gained invaluable experience over the years, and that experience can open doors to new opportunities.

Perhaps there's a creative passion you've always wanted to explore such as writing a book, painting, learning an instrument, or starting a blog. Now is the time to let go of any self-doubt or fear and pursue the creative endeavors that inspire you. Creativity doesn't have an expiration date, and you may find that your most fulfilling projects emerge later in life.

If you've ever considered starting your own business or side hustle, now is the perfect time to do so. You may have the financial stability, knowledge, and network to take a calculated risk in starting something new. Whether it's freelancing, coaching, or offering a service that fills a gap in the market, your 50s can be the perfect time to become an entrepreneur and build something that excites you. More women start businesses in their 50s than at any other time in their life.

Personal growth in your 50s also involves deepening the relationships that matter most and creating new, meaningful connections. As you age, you may find that you are more selective with your time and energy. This means prioritizing relationships that are nurturing, uplifting, and supportive. This is the time to evaluate people in your life. Are your relationships adding value and joy to your life? Or are there connections that drain you, keep you stuck, or hold you back from growing? In your 50s, you may feel more empowered to set boundaries and release relationships that no longer serve you. Surround yourself with those who bring out the best in you.

Never underestimate the power of human connection in your 50s. It can be electric. New people bring fresh perspectives, deep belly laughs, unexpected adventures, and the kind of growth you didn't even know you were craving. I've met more exciting, inspiring souls in my 50s than I did in the decades before. We're gloriously single, brilliantly bold, and completely done with pretending. No fucks given, no masks worn. just raw, real connection with people who have lived, lost, risen, and now choose joy on their own terms. It's not about quantity anymore, it's about the quality of energy you let into your life.

Our 50s are not the end of the road—they are the beginning of an exciting new chapter filled with endless possibilities. This is a time to celebrate your accomplishments, release past limitations, and open yourself up to new opportunities. You have the experience, wisdom, and strength to create the life you've always wanted.

It's never too late to make changes, take risks, and grow. Whether it's learning new skills, forging new relationships, exploring new careers, or simply embracing the freedom to be yourself, the possibilities in your 50s are limitless.

Embrace the adventure ahead. Your 50s are not about slowing down—they're about accelerating into a future filled with passion, purpose, and growth. The best is yet to come.

CHAPTER THIRTEEN: FIFTY IS THE NEW THIRTY

We're hearing all the time that *"50 is the new 30."* It's a phrase that captures the essence of how life in your 50s can feel revitalized, full of energy, and brimming with possibility and now I am living through it, I can say with clarity that this is absolutely true. When I was little, 50 seemed absolutely ancient. I remember my Nanna at 50 in her shapeless smock dresses with patterned resembling duvet covers. Back in the '80s, fifty was seen as old, and women were expected to dress their age in conservative, matronly styles with blue rinses. The mindset was completely different. Gray hair, frumpy cardigans, and sensible shoes were almost a given. Now? We are in the best shape of our lives, well I am. I rocking bold fashion, mini skirts, tight tops, micro strong bikinis, nipple piercings, tattoos and I go clubbing for months on end during summer. I refuse to fade into the background. Fitness, aesthetics, and confidence have completely redefined what 50 looks like today. It's not about aging gracefully anymore. I am all about living fully, looking great, and feeling even better than I did in my 30s. Which by the way, I spent most of fat, bloated, pregnant, and sleep deprived..

As you're reading this book, I congratulate you on being on a similar journey to me and refusing to settle. You've likely learned so much about yourself, your boundaries, and your priorities. You've experienced highs, lows, and everything in between, which means you're entering this phase of life with an incredible amount of wisdom and experience. The beauty of this decade is that it offers a unique opportunity to reframe what aging means and to embrace the idea that you're just getting started.

This stage of life can be one of the most empowering, fulfilling, and exciting chapters yet. In your 30s, you were likely navigating the whirlwind of life's early challenges, building your career, establishing relationships, and figuring out who you really were. You were busy creating your future, taking risks, and learning from mistakes. By the time you hit your 50s, you've had enough time to grow into yourself, gaining invaluable experience in the process.

Your 50s represent a time when your experience has fully matured into wisdom. You know who you are, what you stand for, and what you need to thrive. There's no more pressure to prove yourself to the world. You've lived long enough to appreciate your strengths, and you've likely built resilience through the challenges you've overcome. Whereas in your 30s, you may have doubted yourself or been in the process of figuring things out, in your 50s, you can embrace your achievements without hesitation. This deep sense of self-acceptance comes with maturity, and it allows you to make decisions based on clarity and confidence. A friend recently said she wished she was 30 again. Hell no. I wouldn't go back for anything. I *love* being 50. It's freedom, clarity, and zero tolerance for bullshit. 50 is the new 30 but without the insecurity, the people-pleasing, or the emotional chaos. I've got the confidence, the life experience, the sex appeal, and most importantly, the peace. You couldn't pay me to relive the drama of my younger years. I've earned these years and I'm living them louder.

One of the most exciting aspects of the *"50 is the new 30"* mentality is that it challenges the idea that aging means slowing down. We are living healthier, more active lives than ever. Thanks to advances in healthcare, better access to wellness knowledge, and more awareness of the importance of exercise, many individuals in their 50s are more physically active and healthier than they were in their 30s.

In my 30s, I was certainly active running around after 4 small children but still finding my way to a consistent routine was impossible and I had no energy to go to the gym after sleepless nights and constant runs ro and fro from school and kids clubs. In my 50s, i have found exercise routine that works for you. I get up and I go to the gym. That's it. My working day starts after that. Whether it's yoga, weightlifting, running, or cycling, staying active in your 50s helps maintain strength, flexibility, and cardiovascular health, all of which are essential for feeling youthful and vibrant. For me it's spinning, weightlifting and walking.

You may have fine-tuned your diet to fit your lifestyle and nutritional needs. By your 50s, you know what foods fuel you, what makes you feel good, and how to balance indulgence with healthy habits. Instead of following the latest diet trends, you've learned to listen to your body and give it what it truly needs to feel its best.

By your 50s, you may have learned the importance of sleep, relaxation, and recovery. You realize that rest isn't a luxury, it's a necessity for maintaining both physical and mental health. Taking time to rest, engage in self-care, and recharge is a priority in your life, allowing you to continue thriving with energy and purpose. Now i take a power nap most days even if it's just for half an hour.

Your mental and emotional well-being at 50 is another reason why this age truly feels like the new 30. By now, you've learned how to manage stress, how to navigate life's inevitable ups and downs, and how to honor your emotions without letting them control you.

Your 50s are a time when emotional resilience truly shines. You've learned how to weather life's challenges with grace and wisdom. Where you may have been prone to doubt or insecurity in your 30s, now you approach difficulties with a calm, collected mindset. You've seen enough to know that hard times pass, and you have the strength to rise above them.

In your 30s, you may have still been searching for approval from others. But in your 50s, you've likely come to terms with the fact that true happiness comes from within. Self-acceptance is one of the most empowering gifts of being in your 50s. We're comfortable with who we are, and you're no longer afraid to be unapologetically you.

The sense of independence you've cultivated throughout the years only deepens in your 50s. You're no longer afraid to make decisions that are best for you, even if they don't align with what others expect or want. This newfound confidence gives you the courage to pursue your dreams, speak up for yourself, and live authentically without compromise. When I told people I was writing this book I was inundated with messages from women in the same position as me; bored with their husbands, bored with their husbands, craving more from life, and no longer willing to settle for mediocrity. They were quietly yearning for passion, purpose, and freedom, but didn't know where to begin. That's when I realised this wasn't just my story, it is is our story. A shared awakening. A collective call for something deeper, bolder, and unapologetically true.

As we get older, we tend to become more selective about the relationships we invest in. By your 50s, you've likely cultivated deep, meaningful friendships that bring you joy and support. The friendships and relationships that matter most are often the ones that nurture you, not drain you.One of the most powerful aspects of being in your 50s is that you've likely learned to recognize and let go of toxic relationships. Whether it's friends, family, or romantic partners, you no longer tolerate negativity, drama, or dysfunction. You've learned to protect your peace and prioritize the people who uplift and support you.

Turning 50 doesn't mean slowing down. It means leaning into the next chapter of your life with vitality, confidence, and possibility. We have accumulated wisdom, clarity, and resilience, and we're more prepared than ever to seize new opportunities, redefine our goals, and create the life we want on our terms.

Embrace the idea that 50 is the new 30. Not in the sense of trying to turn back the clock, but in recognizing that the best is yet to come. Our 50s are full of potential, growth, and excitement.

The next chapter is yours to write. One that is rich with experience, wisdom, and the courage to live authentically. So, here's to your 50s: a decade of embracing your power, your vitality, and the boundless opportunities that await you. The future is brighter than ever.

CHAPTER FOURTEEN: LIVE LIFE ON YOUR TERMS

I hate it when people say to me , "I'm too old or "I've missed that opportunity now". Fuck that attitude. What are you? A carton of milk past its sell by date? This idea that you've somehow missed the boat because you hit 50 is one of the most damaging, boring, and frankly, lazy lies we tell ourselves. Your life is yours to live. No one else's definition of success, happiness, or purpose needs to be your own. The freedom to choose who you want to be and how you want to live is one of the most powerful gifts you can give yourself. You get to decide. Do you know what happens at 50?

You wake up.

And for the first time in your life, you get a glimpse of just how much time you've spent being polite. Waiting. Playing small. Doing what was expected and not what you *wanted*. But now? Now you get to choose again. Or for the first time ever.

Let me ask you something: Who told you it was too late? A man? A magazine feature?

Your own fear disguised as logic?

The world is full of people who will happily keep you in a box. And guess what? Most of them aren't even happy in their own lives. So if someone tells you it's too late to start again, change careers, fall in love, leave a dead marriage, dye your hair pink, or sell your house and move to the damn seaside, that says more about *them* than it ever will about you. There is no deadline on desire. On joy. On purpose. You're not too old. You're just *bored* of the bullshit. This is exactly one of the reasons I left my husband.

Here's what no one tells you: the door you've been waiting for someone else to open? It's not locked. It never was. You just have to stop asking permission.

Don't wait for your kids to be okay with it.

Don't wait for your friends to understand.

Don't wait for a man to approve, or for the universe to send a damn sign.

Here's the sign.

Do you want it? Go get it.

Do you regret it? Change it.

You dream of it? Make it real.

And if anyone tells you you've "missed your opportunity," smile politely and go make a new one.

You're not too old. You're in your prime.

You haven't missed your opportunity. You've only just stopped ignoring it.

This life is happening right now. And you don't get another go. So stop waiting. Stop doubting. Stop watering yourself down to make everyone else comfortable.

You're going to die so do it anyway.

.

The key to living life on your terms is embracing the idea that life is short and precious. Every moment is an opportunity to make a choice, create change, and embrace freedom. Don't wait for the perfect time to start living fully. The perfect time is now. You don't need to wait for permission from others or for circumstances to align perfectly. You already have the power to create the life you want.

How many times do I have to drum it in? You have one life to live, and if you haven't done it by now, it's time to embrace the freedom to make it your own. Living life on your terms means choosing happiness, authenticity, and empowerment above all else. It's about letting go of the "shoulds" and "musts" that weigh you down and stepping into a life that feels fulfilling, purposeful, and uniquely yours.

Remember that you are the author of your story. You have the power to shape your life, create new possibilities, and live with freedom and joy. It's time to step into your power and live life fully and fearlessly, exactly the way you've always wanted to. What's the worst thing that could happen? You could die but you're going to anyway eventually. And when I am facing that I want to say I lived a life with purpose and no regrets.

If I had a penny for every time someone said to me,

"Oh, I wish I could do what you've done... you're so brave," I wouldn't need to start over, I'd be bloody minted. But let me tell you the truth they don't want to hear:

It wasn't bravery. It was survival. It was waking up every day in a life that no longer fit and finally deciding that staying small was more terrifying than starting again. It wasn't about courage, it was about reclaiming my right to live. It was knowing that staying where I was felt like slow death. It was refusing to shrink just because it made other people feel safe. It was waking up one day and thinking, *"Is this it?"* And answering, *No. Not for me.*

Brave? No. Scared? Absolutely. But I did it anyway. Because the alternative was waking up ten years later in the same place, with the same ache in my gut, the same restless soul, and no one to blame but myself.

And here's the thing, when people say *"I wish I could..."* What they usually mean is *"I'm not ready to lose the approval I've built my life around."*

They mean *"I don't know who I am without this version of me."*

They mean *"I've confused comfort with happiness."*

And I get it. I really do. I was there once too, sitting at the edge of my life, calling it a seatbelt when it was actually a cage. But no one's coming to rescue you. No magic email, no perfect sign, no man with a better plan. You either jump or get stuck.

Bravery isn't a personality type. It's a *decision.*

Your 50s are when most people are told to settle down and stay quiet. To age gracefully. To disappear. Well, fuck that too. I didn't come this far, survive this much, and learn all I've learned just to fade out politely. Neither did you.

So next time someone tells you how brave you are, or how they *wish* they could do the same, smile. Then tell them the truth. They can do whatever the hell they want to. But they'll have to want their freedom more than their comfort.

Let go of what people think. Choose yourself without apology. Because you're going to die so do it anyway.

CHAPTER FIFTEEN: EMBRACE THE UNKNOWN

Life is a journey that's full of twists, turns, and unexpected detours. While we often try to control the path ahead, the truth is that uncertainty is inevitable. Whether it's a new job, a relationship, a move to a different city, or even an uncharted creative endeavor, the unknown is constantly present. And yet, it's the unknown that holds the potential for growth, adventure, and transformation.

In a world that thrives on planning, certainty, and predictability, embracing the unknown might feel unsettling at first. But when you allow yourself to enter uncertainty with courage and trust, you unlock a world of possibilities. The human brain is wired for comfort. We naturally seek predictability because it offers a sense of security. Knowing what to expect provides peace of mind, and following routines keeps us feeling grounded. But the downside of this comfort is that we can become stuck in cycles of predictability that prevent us from experiencing new things. We become complacent, and the excitement of possibility fades.

The unknown, on the other hand, offers us something far more profound: freedom. When you step out of your comfort zone and embrace uncertainty, you're free from the limitations of what's already known. You open yourself to new experiences, new people, and new opportunities. Sure, there might be risks, but there's also incredible potential for transformation.

The unknown isn't a threat. It's a blank canvas waiting for you to paint a new masterpiece.

One of the biggest challenges of embracing the unknown is learning to trust yourself. When faced with uncertainty, many of us doubt our abilities, our decisions, or our capacity to handle whatever comes our way. Self-doubt creeps in, and we start questioning if we're equipped to navigate the unpredictable.

But here's the key: You've been through challenges before, and you've come out stronger. Think back to a time when you faced uncertainty—whether it was a major life change or a personal challenge—and consider how you handled it. You survived, adapted and learned. You grew through the experience, even if it didn't unfold as you expected.

Trusting yourself means recognizing that you are capable of handling whatever life throws your way. It's about letting go of the need for certainty and embracing the fact that you are resourceful, resilient, and powerful. When you trust yourself, you trust the process of life, knowing that even in moments of doubt or fear, you'll find a way to navigate through it.

The unknown is often where new beginnings are born. It's where the seeds of change are planted, and where life unfolds in ways you never imagined. If you never took a step into the unknown, you would miss out on the vast, beautiful possibilities that lie on the other side of fear.

Think about the times in your life when you made a leap of faith, be it a new job, a new relationship, a new home and the doors it opened for you. At first, it might have felt daunting. The uncertainty of those moments might have left you feeling nervous or unsure. But eventually, you saw the magic in the newness. The unknown led you to new opportunities, deeper connections, and richer experiences.

Embracing the unknown doesn't mean jumping in without a plan or being reckless. It means trusting that sometimes the best things in life happen when you take a step into the unfamiliar when you open yourself to the potential of what's to come.

Fear is often one of the biggest obstacles to embracing the unknown. The fear of failure, rejection, or the fear of making the "wrong" choice can paralyze us, keeping us stuck in the safety of what we already know. But fear doesn't have to hold us back. Instead, it can be a powerful indicator that we're on the verge of something significant.

When fear arises, it's a sign that we are stepping out of our comfort zone and into a new realm of growth. Instead of letting fear dictate your decisions, use it as fuel to advance. Fear means you're growing. It means you're moving toward something new, something that has the potential to change your life in ways you can't yet see.

The key is to acknowledge the fear without letting it control you. Recognize that uncertainty and fear are natural parts of the journey, and that they don't define your ability to succeed. By embracing the unknown, you show yourself that you have the courage to take risks and the resilience to navigate whatever comes your way.

One of the most powerful ways to embrace the unknown is to live fully in the moment. Often, our fear of the unknown is rooted in worry about the future. What will happen if things don't go according to plan, or if we make the wrong choice? But by focusing on the here and now, we free ourselves from the burden of future uncertainties.

Living in the present means trusting that the answers you need will come at the right time. It means enjoying the journey, even if you don't have all the details figured out. When you stop trying to control every aspect of your future and let go of the need for certainty, you create space for spontaneity, adventure, and joy.

Take time each day to center yourself in the present moment. Whether through meditation, mindful breathing, or simply focusing on what's happening right now, staying grounded in the present allows you to move through life with more ease, peace, and acceptance of the unknown.

Letting go is a powerful way to embrace the unknown. So often, we cling to the past. Old stories, regrets, or outdated goals because they feel familiar and safe. But in doing so, we hold ourselves back from the future. To embrace the unknown, we must be willing to release what no longer serves us.

Letting go means being open to change. It means shedding the weight of old beliefs or expectations that keep you anchored in the past. Whether it's letting go of the need to control outcomes or releasing relationships or situations that no longer align with your growth, letting go creates space for new experiences.

We don't need to know every detail to move forward. Trust that when you let go of the need for certainty, the universe will bring you exactly what you need when the time is right. Embrace the mystery of life, and trust that the unknown is leading you toward something greater than you can imagine.

Finally, to embrace the unknown is to trust the flow of life. Life is not always linear, and it doesn't always follow the neat, tidy plans we make. It's a winding, ever-changing path filled with surprises, challenges, and beautiful moments of serendipity. The unknown is the river that carries us forward, guiding us to places we never imagined we'd go.

When you allow yourself to flow with life without rigid expectations or the need for constant control you enter a state of grace and ease. You begin to see challenges as opportunities for growth and learn to navigate uncertainty with curiosity and confidence.

Embracing the flow of life means letting go of resistance. It means trusting that life is unfolding exactly as it should, and that every detour and every twist has something valuable to offer.

In conclusion, embracing the unknown is not just about stepping outside your comfort zone; it's about seeing the beauty and potential that uncertainty holds. When you let go of the need for control, you open yourself up to the magic of new experiences, opportunities, and growth.

The unknown doesn't have to be scary, it's where life's greatest adventures await. So, trust the journey, embrace the uncertainty, and allow yourself to be guided by the possibilities that lie ahead. Life is an unfolding adventure, and the beauty lies in the mystery of what's to come and the adventure of a lifetime

CHAPTER SIXTEEN :   WRITE A BUCKET LIST

You're going to die so do it anyway. There's no better time to write a bucket list and start living it. I have done many things, such as going to Norway to the tip of the North Pole to see the Northern lights. I have climbed a mountain which was terrifying but exhilarating. I have seen multiple Broadway shows in New York, I have stood outside the Sydney Opera House and cried, I have snorkeled in the Great Barrier Reef. I have eaten sushi in Japan. I have published more than one book, I have raised wonderful, kind and intelligent children. I have gone clubbing until sunrise three days in a row (that was my 50th birthday celebration). I have had one night stands, I have lived abroad, taken a month off work multiple times to sit on a beach. I have taken burlesque lessons, I have taken magic mushrooms, I have been whale watching in Spain and been to technology shows in Japan and Hong Kong.I taught myself graphic design and how to use AI.I have experienced sunrise and sunset more times than I can remember. I had sex on the beach (and we're not talking about the tacky cocktails). I have been on a spiritual retreat, I have been to a tea ceremony in Japan, I have watched my cat give birth and raised her kittens. I have experienced the awe-inspiring phenomenon of a total solar eclipse, in a place where it's most visible in Regents Park in London whilst enjoying a champagne picnic breakfast. I already make a living from something I am passionate about. I have created fashion shows in 3 countries,I have had conversations with famous people through my work as a journalist. I have taken myself to parties and networking events alone. I have been on cruises, I have had dinner on the Orient Express, feeling like I was in an Agatha Christie novel. I have explored castles and beautiful stately homes steeped in history which I love. I learned to play the drums and the clarinet when I was younger. I have learnt to speak French and German. I know how to meditate, I have ridden in a helicopter and done a motorbike riding course. I have shadowed the police and ambulance service for a day for newspaper feature reporting. I have written a song and released it as a single.I regularly bathe under the full moon in the sea. I have written a television programme and I have appeared on television many times. I had my writing published every month for the last 30 years. I have got tattoos and piercings. given birth six times which is my ultimate greatest achievement. I almost died twice, but I didn't and did it anyway.

In essence, up until this point in my life, I have lived spontaneously and allowed myself to make an unplanned decision that has to be an unforgettable adventure, just for the sake of joy. Actually, that's all pretty impressive.

Here's my list of , however, of what I have yet to achieve

1 **Travel to All Seven Continents**

Explore the diverse cultures, landscapes, and wildlife of places like Antarctica, &

South America . I have visited 5 continents, two more to go.

2 **Take luxury train Trip Across multiple countries**

I want to explore hidden gems and iconic destinations. I would love to drive East

to West Coast USA

3. **Volunteer Abroad**

I love animals and want to experience the magic of connecting with intelligent,

playful creatures in their natural habitat and hopefully not get eaten by them

4.   Hike the Inca Trail to Machu Picchu

I want to challenge myself physically and mentally by trekking through one of the

most famous trails in the world.

5.   Take a Hot Air Balloon Ride

I want to soar peacefully over a beautiful landscape like the Serengeti, Napa

Valley, or Cappadocia.

.

6.   See the Great Wall of China

I want to walk along one of the most iconic man-made wonders in the world, marveling at its history and magnitude.

.

7. Stay in an Overwater Bungalow

I want to live in luxury for a week on crystal-clear waters, in a beautiful destination like the Maldives or Bora Bora with a butler attending to my every needs.

8. Take a Cooking Class in Italy or France

I want to learn the secrets of Italian or French cuisine from a local chef and cook up a feast. Ironic because I actually hate cooking, I find it a chore.

9. Go on a Wildlife Safari in Africa

I want to observe the magnificent animals of the African savannah in their natural environment, like lions, elephants, and giraffes.

10. Visit All 50 U.S. States

I have been to the east and west coast but there's so much to explore in between. I want to experience the diversity of the United States, from Alaska's wild terrain to the vibrant culture of New Orleans.

11. Ride in a Private Jet

I want the luxury and comfort of flying in a private jet, making travel even more exciting and take tons of instagram pics. Just because.

12. Take a Cruise Around the World

I want to spend 6 months on a long voyage to multiple countries and islands, exploring new destinations every few days.

13. Go Horseback Riding on the Beach

I am scared of horses but i relish the freedom of riding a horse along the coastline, wind in my hair, the ocean as my backdrop. I am thinking Wuthering Heights.

14 Spend a Night in an Ice Hotel

I hate the cold but I want to stay in a hotel made entirely of ice and snow, enjoying the beauty of an icy wonderland

15. **Fall in love and have a beautiful romance, wild sex and endless laughs.**

16. **Buy everything on my Amazon Wishlist**

CONCLUSION

You ARE going to die. So do it anyway.

Turning 50 is a beautiful milestone. Fuck the 35 year old if you want and it makes you feel alive. Perk yourself up with some facial aesthetics if that's what you want and it makes you feel good. Wear a tight dress with the cleavage showing. Dance on the beach until dawn. Tell your sexist boss to go fuck themselves. There's no point in looking back on your life and dwelling on your regrets. Look back with pride at how far you've come and look forward with excitement. You've earned the wisdom you carry and now you're in a position to truly step into your power. You're not just "getting older", you're evolving into the most authentic, unapologetic version of yourself. More confident, more certain, and more attuned to what truly matters to you. So be proud of this stage. It's one where you've got the chance to shape your world, share your gifts, and live out your wisdom like never before.

Your voice, perspective and presence are treasures. Don't let anyone, including yourself forget that. This is your life so own it majestically and unapologetically. Let's stop pretending we have all the time in the world. We don't.

You're going to die. I'm going to die. Everyone you know is. That might sound brutal, but it's the truth and the most liberating truth there is.

Because once you stop fearing death, you start living. At 50, something shifts. You realise you've got less time ahead than behind. That can either scare the life out of you or it can light a fire so fierce it burns away every excuse, every fear, every "maybe next year."

And I'll tell you that my life is so much better and not one part of it came from being fearless. It came from doing things despite the fear. From choosing discomfort over regret. From knowing that time is the only thing I'll never get back so I won't waste another second waiting to feel ready.

We're 50. We've survived heartbreak, courtroom drama, disappointment, menopause, stretch marks, betrayal, boredom, and a thousand other things that tried to break you. And yet here we are. Glorious. Alive. Awake.

So stop asking if you're too old, too late, too loud, too much. You are right on time.

Tell the truth. Take up space. Say yes. Say no. Say *fuck it*. You're not here to please. You're here to live.

And you don't need to explain a single thing to anyone who doesn't get it. Because here's the deal: you're going to die one day. That's inevitable. What isn't inevitable is whether you'll die with stories, memories, and a heart that's been fully used or if you'll die with dreams still locked inside you.So choose the stories. Choose unbothered.

Slide into the next chapter wild-eyed and laughing, whispering, *"Fuck me, that was fun."* We have maybe 25 years left if we're lucky. And those years are ours.. Not for shrinking. Not for waiting. Not for apologising. They are for doing it boldly, loudly, joyfully, defiantly.

You've already done the hardest part: you woke up. You left the old life behind. You chose yourself. And now? Now it's game on. No one is coming to save you. No one is handing out gold stars. There is no prize for being polite or invisible

I've survived the shit most people don't talk about. And now, I'm not just just alive, I'm awake. And so are you.

Do it all.

Because the only thing worse than dying is not living while you're still here.

Printed in Dunstable, United Kingdom